HUMAN, HELP THYSELF!

Natural Solutions

for

Stress of Body, Mind & Spirit

by

Rev. Lena Sheehan, D/M, ND, CHt.

A. K.A. Eileen Sheehan)

I would like to express my sincerest appreciation to my students around the world. It is their constant curiosities and dedication to enlightenment and advancement that propels me forward with my own personal growth.

AUTHOR'S MESSAGE

WHEN I WAS FIRST APPROACHED to write this book, my initial reaction was, "What can I write about that has not already been covered?" In my opinion, the topic of stress and its management has been in print over and over and over again by numerous authors; too many to count. Some of these books have become national best sellers, while others are just sitting on the shelf. But, never-the-less, they are out there and in print.

While in conversation with my students, I was reminded of the many times I had repeated the same thing until it had finally registered with them. We spoke about the fact that 99 people may be making a statement about the same matter, yet it takes the 100th person speaking about that matter before the subject catches their attention and is digested and perceived.

My students pointed out the many times I had stated that we all do not resonate with the same vibration and may reject from one what we accept from another; so, I agreed to write this book in hopes that I might be the 100th person for those of you who have experienced the 99 people before me.

What write about is not new. Then, the worlds of metaphysics and holistic practices are not new. They are as old as time. The New Age is the Old Age returning. Therefore, it stands to reason that there will be literature about these ancient realities in abundance. Yet, as old as they are and as widely covered in literature as these subjects may be, there is still a large populous of people who are only now discovering or beginning to accept and understand how to manage stress of body, mind and spirit with metaphysics, spiritual and holistic methods. Stress management of your body, mind and spirit has become a national topic. The newsstands and bookstores are filled with topics focusing on the subject. Even so, there are people who either do not understand the benefits or cannot comprehend the necessity for managing the stress they are experiencing. It is with these people in mind that I have chosen to write this book. I have combined pragmatic information with metaphysical, spiritual, and holistic information with the intention of providing you with enough of an informative foundation in all areas to afford you the opportunity for a well-balanced, stress free existence.

There is a lot of valuable information packed in this little book. My suggestion is that you read it more than once and use it as a reference when needed. Each time you open this book you may discover or comprehend something that you may have overlooked during your previous reading. Often, we recognize and absorb only when it is needed or when we are ready to accept the information before us.

STRESS

"THINGS IN LIFE ARE not good or bad, it is what you think they are."
William Shakespeare

I FOCUS ON THE TOPIC of stress because I believe that it is at the core of most of your issues and diseases. If you can limit stress in your life through understanding, you will see a major reduction in other negatives. According to Webster's Dictionary of the English Language, stress is "a state of bodily or mental tension, resulting from factors that tend to alter existent equilibrium."

So, what determines that state? If you stand ten people in a room and have the walls fall around them, all ten are apt to give you a varied version of the same experience. Some will feel stressed and act frenzied, while others will be disturbed that it occurred and ponder on the reason it happened. Yet, others will look at those around them who are upset and frenzied and ask them, "What's the big deal?"

Stress is the result of a person's interpretation of a situation, be it their environmental surroundings, emotional reactions or the demands and changes in the body.

It is virtually impossible to eliminate exposure to every situation that has potential to cause you stress, but you can work on avoiding them to the best of your abilities. And, at those times when you cannot avoid it and you are exposed to stress, you can change how you respond to the situation, therefore minimizing or actually neutralizing the impact it may have had on your emotional, spiritual, or physical wellbeing. Stress is an ongoing and never-ending part of your life, but it does not have to become your way of life! Just think about it; if you clean up your environment and make it as stress-free as possible, while you shift your way of thinking toward those unavoidable stressors, you can enjoy a more happy and healthy lifestyle.

How unfortunate that so many people put the

nurturing of their bodies, their minds, and their spirits at the last of their list of priorities. Cleaning up the environment, be it a physical, emotional, or mental clean up, is something many people just do not consider important. They are focused on the demands of day to day living, while ignoring the vital messages that their bodies are giving. A few years ago, I owned and operated a stress management center and I found the amount of people who would stand at the door and laugh, stating that they needed stress management, but do nothing about it to be staggering. We were constantly having to educate from square one. The point that they were missing was that stress puts a real demand on their bodies every day; and how they deal with this stress will determine how effectively they perform their daily tasks; be those tasks emotional, physical, or spiritual. The effects that stress can have on your total being is not a joke to be laughed at and the sooner people recognize this, the sooner we will all enjoy a healthier and more stable lifestyle.

Something that creates stress is called a "stressor." It can be of a mental-emotional nature, a physical-biochemical nature or an environmental-biological nature. Your exposure to some or all these stressors is common and sometimes unavoidable. Because of this, it is up to you, the individual, to interpret these stressors in a manner that will give you an opportunity to respond in a minimizing or neutralizing way. Thus, avoiding any negative impact they could potentially have on you.

You have an automatic biological response to stress that has been with mankind since his beginning. It is most commonly referred to as your fight or flight response. All creatures possess the fight or fight response and there has always been a viable purpose for it through history. It has proven to be a lifesaver in more than one occasion.

Sometimes the responses your body had to stress by way of the flight or fight syndrome go unrecognized as such. The best-known responses are the shifting and changing of the normal functioning of your respiratory system, cardiovascular system, metabolic system, and your hormone levels. You could also experience changes in your enzymes, GI functioning and urinary system. Although these shifts and changes were important back when man was fleeing from predators when fighting for survival, today these very same alterations in your body that are induced by stressors can hurt you instead of help.

It is unfortunate, but your body can not

differentiate between a harmful and a non-harmful stressor, therefore it is up to your mind to do the differentiating and then trigger the response of your body. This is where the problem appears. Too many people today are not recognizing a stressor and therefore do not direct their body in the proper response. This ignorance is causing them to unwittingly be destroyed by the very same bodily functions that were intended to save their life!

Although many stressors are real, there are just as many (if not more) that are perceived.

When your body senses a stressor (real or perceived) it will respond automatically by preparing and mobilizing for a physical conflict or a sudden retreat from that stressor or situation. Your hormones will surge, and your nervous system prepares for either the fight or the flight. Your heart rate increases and your breathing speeds up; which allows more oxygen into your body. Your muscles are made ready for action and your blood pressure surges as your blood rushes to them. When your body's metabolic rate shifts into high gear in this manner, you are experiencing Oxidative Stress.

When Oxidative Stress occurs, your digestion is temporarily placed on hold and your blood clotting mechanisms are activated to allow your body to focus on the task at hand. Now, in a real physical threat this would be wonderful! But what if the threat is not physical? What if the threat is something with an emotional base such as traffic jams or conflicts at work or arguments with your loved ones, etc.? It is important that you understand how life threatening a steady and constant exposure to this type of stress can be or, at the very least, the years it can take from your life.

Prolonged and repeated emotional-mental stress can produce the same physical responses as physical stress and can contribute to one or more of the following: cardiovascular disease, gastro-intestinal dysfunction, immune deficiency, reproductive difficulty, sleep and memory loss and premature aging. And this is just to name a few!

Here is the good news. You Are in Control.

By this I mean that you have the power to determine how stressed out you will allow yourself to be in any given situation. Let me repeat that. YOU have the power to a determine how stress out you will allow yourself to be in any given situation.

When you take control and determine not to allow a stressor to affect you, your heart rate and breathing will slow down, your blood pressure will lower, your muscles will relax, and the metabolism of your body will normalize. So, why aren't people just taking it easy and de-stressing? That is a good question.

One of the main reasons, in my opinion, is that many people simply are not aware of the stressors in their lives or possibly are aware that they are there, but are not fully knowledgeable of the harmful effects these stressors can potentially have. I have listed a few here. See how many you perceived as genuinely hazardous to your health.

1] Cigarette smoke, including second hand smoke.
2] Excess fat intake
3] Excessive stress
4] Radiation and certain medications
5] Synthetic food additives
6] Asbestos and similar materials
7] Environmental pollutants in the air, food, and water
8] Household cleansers
9] Pesticides
10] Charcoal smoke/barbecues
11] Plastics
12] Excessive exercise
13] Caffeine
14] Loud music
15] Telephones
16] Commuting to work

Stress is a common denominator in many illnesses; from something as simple as a headache to a more serious disease (dis-ease) such as heart disease. When we study the physiological changes that are created during a stressful situation, it is easy to see the link between your mind, stress, and the illness.

Let's take a moment to look at your heart's response to various situation. It will pound when you experience anxiety, it will skip a beat when you are fearful, and it sinks when you are disappointed.

Everyone is aware, intuitively, of the relationship between the emotional stress of your body and the functioning of your heart. Although, from what I have learned, there is still some controversy amongst doctors as to the role mental stress plays on heart disease, I feel the evidence that your mind plays a role in the development of heart disease is growing. One possible reason for this deduction is that depressed, or overly stressed people seem to be more likely to engage in self-destructive behaviors such as smoking. (Did you know that smoking appears to be more prevalent with women?) Another reason is that depression or stress stimulates the sympathetic nerves, which in turn can increase your heart rate which causes your blood vessels to constrict and your blood pressure to elevate.

Your speech behavioral pattern is a strong indication of whether you are experiencing excessive stress and hostility. Below are a few questions for you to ask yourself to help you determine if you are displaying excessive stress through hostility.

Ask yourself these questions:

1.When you speak, is it in a loud, rapid, and forceful manner?

2.Do you have a tendency to interrupt others when they are speaking so that you can give them input, or even change the subject matter?

3.When you do not agree with a person, are you forceful or argumentative?

4.Do you tend to make critical, cynical, or rude remarks to or about people or things?

If you answered yes to any or all of these questions, then your behavior is risking your health with high levels of hostility.

Since hostility often goes unrecognized and untreated, I think we should look at it just a little more closely.

The following is a self-test. Circle yes or no to
answer each question:

1. Do you check out the baskets ahead of you when you are standing in a supermarket express checkout line, counting their items to be certain they have not exceeded the line limit?]

2. If you discover the person in front of you has exceeded the checkout line limit, do you say something to them about it?

3. If a cashier gives you the wrong change, do you automatically get into a huff or assume it was done deliberately?

4. Do you dwell on things?

5. Do you get impatient waiting for elevators or press the buttons in them repeatedly with the intent of making the elevator move more quickly?

6. Do you allow life's little daily frustrations to stay with you, accumulate and blend with the bigger ones?

7. Do you take your work home with you?

8. When someone keeps you waiting, do you greet him or her with criticism or angry words?

9. When your hair or nails are not done the way you want them to be, do you fuss and fume about it right on into the following day or days? (Yes, men worry about those things too!)

10. Does your pulse quicken or your jaw clench when you disagree or argue with someone?

11. Do you experience road rage?

12. If someone pulls in front of you in a drive-in line (I.E. bank or fast food restaurant) do you shout at them or honk your horn in disapproval?

13. When someone mistreats you, do you plan methods of getting back at him or her simply for principal?

14. When you find yourself unhappy with someone else, do you recall and/or bring up old hurts that they have inflicted upon you?

If you answered yes to three or less, you are in pretty good shape. If you answered yes to four and up to eight, you are experiencing hostility that may lead to a serious illness. If you answered yes to nine or more, you are in what is referred to as the "hot zone." This is a dangerous level of anger, cynicism and aggression that will increase the possibility of the destruction of your health and/or relationships. If you are at this level, then suggest that you take the necessary steps to get the help you need to correct this situation.

Allowing yourself to remain in a stressful situation for an extended period cannot only break down your physical body, but it also has an effect on your emotional body.

A panic attack is another symptom of some type of stress and can occur out of nowhere; sometimes lasting for several minutes before it subsides. If you don't know how to recognize a panic attack, the symptoms are: chest pains, heart palpitations, sweating, nausea, dizziness, sensations of choking or smothering, numbness or tingling and a sense of losing control and possibly a fear of dying. There is even a possibility of a temporary loss of consciousness. People who experience attacks of this nature tend to live in constant fear of the next one. What a horrendous cycle to be in!

The world is seeing more and more single parent households today. As a result, we are noticing increased stress on the child as well as the parent. This stress not only affects them on a personal level, but it trickles out to the work place and school environments. Over-crowded day care facilities and school classrooms, plus latch key situations, are prime contributions. Not only do these conditions cause stress in themselves on the children and the teachers, but they can bring on a sense of guilt for the parent; which is also a form of stress.

Speaking of children, it has been stated that one in six couples is either infertile or has extreme difficulty in conceiving; and the numbers are growing! In spite of the recent breakthrough in fertility treatment, I am told that about half of the couples who are seeking medical treatments still do not conceive. I question if the cause could it be more emotionally rooted than a physical situation? We know that infertility causes stress, depression, and anxiety. But could it be possible that stress, depression, and anxiety could also inhibit conceiving? In my opinion, absolutely!

In my years as a spiritual medium, medical intuitive, holistic naturopathic healer, nutrition specialist, energy worker and hypnotherapist, I have come into contact and worked with several fertility cases that were solved primarily with the use of my services. In some cases, I worked mainly with past life regression and hypnotherapy to aid in the woman's ability to overcome deep rooted emotional/sub-conscious obstacles so that she could conceive and not abort after the conception and in other cases I simply did energy work on the woman who was experiencing a pregnancy that was considered high risk to aid in her maintaining a sense of balance. My belief is that family oriented, infertile women are far more likely to be depressed than fertile women are. This condition should not be taken lightly. I feel it should be viewed as

seriously as cancer, heart disease and AIDS.

So far, I have been mentioning stress and its relationship to very serious diseases, but how about stress and the common cold? Had you put those two together? I recall reading an article in my travels about how British research has provided evidence that psychological stress can increase susceptibility to cold viruses. It stated that four-hundred men and women participated in a study after first undergoing a medical examination, blood testing and psychological questionnaires that contained questions such as the number of major stressful events in their lives over the past year (I.E. death in the family, job pressures, etc.) and their current level of negative feelings (I.E. sadness, irritations, etc.); then, all of the subjects were given nose drops. Some contained one of five cold viruses. Their blood was tested for cold virus anti-bodies and they were monitored for signs such as sneezing and stuffy-runny noses, sore throats, and coughs. The researchers found that those under stress were far more likely to become infected with the virus and

develop the symptoms.

Studies also indicate that small, everyday

hassles and positive experiences influence your immune system. This is a great argument for relieving stress from the work environment! Just think of the increased quality of production that could occur from a simple thing like the fact that the work force is healthy and feeling good.

It is not just your heart and your respiratory

system that can be affected by stress. Stress can also raise havoc on your GI (gastro-intestinal) system. Many adults have irritable colon, spastic colon, spastic colitis, or another type of functional bowl disease. Do you have Irritable Bowel Syndrome and not know it? The symptoms of IBS (Irritable Bowel Syndrome) are: severe abdominal cramps, bloating, constipation alternating with diarrhea, pellet like stools and mucus in the stool or a sensation of incomplete emptying after a bowel movement. These symptoms may not be constant and may come and go. Although there are many factors that are believed to contribute to IBS, stress is a major consideration as was determined through several tests using psychotherapy and/or hypnosis. But it doesn't stop there. Other gastro-intestinal disorders including Esophageal Reflux and Peptic ulcers, as well as skin disorders such as Psoriasis and eczema have been associated with stress.

Disease equals dis-ease and it is around you all of the time. It is your immune system that determines whether to allow the dis-ease to enter your body, settle in, develop roots, and then thrive. If your immune system is healthy, you can wander through a contaminated area without being infected. Keeping the effects of stress on your body down to a minimum is one way to help boost your immune system and maintain a healthy lifestyle.

THE SPIRITUAL SIDE OF THINGS

NOW THAT YOU HAVE A pretty good idea of the havoc stress can play in your life it is time to start learning to identify it and decide how to handle it. Since I am a spiritual and evangelistic minister and a medium as well as a holistic practitioner and hypnotherapist, my approach to handling stress and the well-being of a human is through traditional, spiritual, metaphysical, and holistic means.

The term metaphysics refers to being out of the normally viewed scope or realm of things. (meta- [out of] –physics) In this book I will be focusing on thoughts, ideas and concepts that date back centuries, but have only just recently been reintroduced to society to the point of being accepted and considered as normal. I feel it is necessary to have a clear understanding and acceptance of metaphysics along with a sense of comfort with your spiritual side as well and good solid pragmatic information in order to keep your body-mind-spirit in a balanced and stress-less condition.

Therefore, I will be approaching all in this book. The next thing that I want to discuss with you is your own personal spirit guide. Your acceptance, recognition, and labeling of such depends greatly on your spiritual, cultural, and religious upbringing, for which I feel is a topic for an entire book all by itself and therefore will not broach it in this one except to state that the following is what I believe and know (through personal experience) to be true: Everyone has his or her own personal spirit guide(s). Along with your own guide there are other Master guides who assist as well. Urla-Ra is my own personal spirit guide and a Master teacher for the planet. I connected with him fully in 1983. Since that time, he has been my mentor and my friend.

In the early 1990's, I received the message while meditating to "Plant the seeds of light that they may grow into valleys of rays". (Light meaning knowledge) It was at this time, trusting the guidance I was receiving, that I began to accumulate and record the information being given to me and sharing it with others. I have been sharing knowledge and working with Urla-Ra in assisting others with their own personal development ever since.

When you make the choice to study spirituality and metaphysics with me, either in person or by correspondence, you are also making the choice of studying under the guidance of Urla-Ra. I am a liaison for information to flow from him to you. The source of Urla-Ra's energy is called the "Council of 12". This is not a council of 12 spirits, but a council of the vibration of the number 12. The last incarnation that Urla-Ra spent on the planet earth was with Jesus the Christ. You will find the energy influence of my wonderful master teacher in the writing of this book. As a master teacher, Urla-Ra has earned the right not to have to incarnate but will do so if the necessity of mankind requires his presence physically. Until that time, I relish and enjoy my connection with Urla-Ra and his teachings and I encourage you to take the time to become more familiar with your own guides. Through the ages there have been recordings and lore about mystics and sages and their connection with the universal energies and Infinite Creator, the Creator. It has been the general belief that this great connection and these wonderful mysteries are available only to a select few. Most of the mainstream religions are very firm in their doctrines that only the pillars of their churches are privileged enough to have the connections that would afford them the ability to communicate with the Holy Realm, giving them the ability to manifest through prayer. It seems the consensus is that if you are not attached to a church and are not ranking high on their ladder of succession in this church but are in some way practicing or owning these powers, then you are sinning or going against Infinite Creator's laws. I can't tell you how many people who Natural Solutions for Stress of Body, Mind & Spirit have gotten to know me on a social level and enjoying my company immensely, prior to knowing what I do, have hesitated at my doorstep in dismay after discovering my vocation. A product of the mainstream consensus, they genuinely liked me, but feared that they were entering a den of iniquity.

If you look up the meaning of the word

religion in Webster's New Dictionary of the English Language, it reads as follows: *re-lig-ion 1.a. An organized system of beliefs and rituals centering on a supernatural being or beings. B. Adherence to such a system. 2. A belief upheld and* *pursued with zeal and devotion [<religio, bond between a human and the Infinite Creators].*

In other words, a religion, whether it is a mainstream or some little church on the corner or a steady gathering in someone's living room, is an organized belief system that is based on the information and knowledge believed to be the truth by that particular group. This is why you find so many varieties of religions on this planet. Yet they all lead back to the one Creator.

It is my belief that the One Creator, Infinite Creator, did not reserve the holy privileges to just a few but has made these gifts available to all. Isn't it stated that we are all Infinite Creator's children? It is also my belief that the mainstream religions, at some point, lost sight of the original teachings, either due to a few who were trying to control the masses or due to someone misunderstanding the true meaning of the information or perhaps there was a flaw in translation from one language to another.

If you turn to the King James Version of the Holy Bible, you will find that there is evidence through the teaching of the Apostle Paul in Corinthians 1:12-13, about the fact that we all have abilities available to us. The readings state quite clearly that we are all, in some way, given gifts and have within our grasp the connection to the universal creative energies and manifestation. The key is to discover which method of connection is best for you. For most, it is through the power of prayer.

Prayer is speaking to Infinite Creator (or stating your intent) and meditation is listening for the answer (or allowing the energies to flow and meld). Through prayer and meditation, you can control, ease, or eliminate the effects of stressors all in your life.

Through prayer and meditation, you are also able to manifest and create things for yourself and others. On this note, I feel it is important to point out that because we are living in a free will zone and your viewpoint of what is right and perfect for someone you love may not be equivalent to that person's viewpoint of what is right and perfect for him or her, it is important that you acquire his or her permission prior to your performing either prayer or manifestation for that person. You should be careful to respect the fact that others may not desire in their reality what you feel they should desire. There are times when people will appeal to the Higher Self of the ones they love rather than go to the person himself or herself; either because they are unreachable or blocked in some way. This is perfectly acceptable, providing that you can move past your own ego and be certain that you have contacted and received permission from that person's higher self and not made it up because it is what you desire.

Since we are all individuals, the necessity to honor someone's divine right to utilize free will is important. This means that life and spiritual beliefs may not be perceived in the same manner. Just look at the religious wars that are being fought and led by the many versions of scriptures, each proclaiming to hold the absolute "truth" and you will see what I mean. A spiritual person acknowledges his or her fellow man's right to free will and does not judge or condemn someone for thinking and believing differently. Just think how much less stressful it would be to not worry about whether you have been successful with imposing your beliefs on someone and just allowing them to live and let live. I have seen, more than once, that an individual who leads by nonjudgmental example instead of by judgmental force will often reach the appeal of the persons he/she is seeking, and they will follow most willingly, by their own free will.

When you are praying, you are communing with the manifestation gifts of Infinite Creator. One of the hardest obstacles that many of the people I work with have with this is the concept that it is our divine right to receive. Infinite Creator did not create lack, we did! It is Infinite Creator's plan that every human has access to all of the wonderful abundance that is available in our vast universal existence. You are not being greedy. I repeat... There is abundance enough for everyone and partaking in the abundance does not make you greedy! It is yours by divine right. The great Master
Jesus stated, "Ask and ye shall receive." Ask for it,
remain open for it and expect it.

Keeping this factor in mind; it is not necessary to beg or plead for Infinite Creator to grant you something. This is the same as saying you are afraid that it won't happen. The fact is that it happened the instant that you requested it in Infinite Creator's plane, but it is up to you to allow it to manifest itself in the earth plane. This is where your free will comes into play. Are you open to receive it? Do you believe you are worthy of it or are you fearful that you are in some way non-deserving? Let's remember that fear is a negative emotion. First you must be comfortable and "know" that you are indeed deserving of all the good that Infinite Creator has placed in this bountiful universe. Remember that man created lack, not Infinite Creator.

Once you have come to grasp this truth, it may be necessary to retrain your subconscious, which is the computer of your mind and has stored in it all the truths and falsehoods ever whispered to your essence throughout the ages. To do this, start by stating the affirmation that it is so, or giving thanks to Infinite Creator in advance for what you are about to receive into your reality, as well as for what you have already been blessed to have already received. Then continue as if it has already happened and is on its way. I equate it to ordering something from a catalog or the internet. You decide what you want, place your order, expend the energy of money, and await its arrival with total faith that it is coming. If you put those same actions of faith into manifestation of other things (with desire energy replacing money energy) just imagine what you can achieve!

When you express affirmations and gratitude, you are expressing positive vibrations that will lead to the desired results. If, for some reason, you do not receive what you have prayed for, I suggest that you examine your inner being for negative thoughts and doubts that may have blocked it from coming to you.

There are times when your subconscious seems resistant to this reprogramming. This is probably due to such deep-rooted feelings and programming that it may be necessary to take some time to release them before you can continue. This can be done through hypnosis or simply by doing

the following clearing:

I am sorry for any experiences that I may have had in this lifetime or in lifetimes past that have caused me to feel unworthy or angry with myself or ___(you fill in)___. I love myself for the special spiritual being that I am, just as I am. I forgive myself for any shortcomings that I may have or any wrong doings that I may have done in this lifetime and for any shortcomings or any wrong doings that I may have had in lifetimes past. I am truly sorry and ask that Infinite Creator forgives me also. I thank Infinite Creator for this precious gift of life and the ability to make the changes that are needed within myself in order to be a better vessel to receive your wondrous gifts.

I do this now.

If you find that you have only been positive and have exercised ultimate faith and have done the clearing either by hypnosis or the above method, yet still did not receive what you had prayed for, know that everything is in Divine Order and as it should be. This is a time for acceptance and re-evaluation of your desires. There are times when we do not see the whole picture and limit ourselves with our desires and this may have been such a time. Another explanation is Karma. You may be obligated to pay a certain debt in accordance to the laws of the universe and your desire that is being prayed for would alter that obligation. Again, trust that things are as they should be and ask for what is right and perfect for you to occur. Even paying back a karmic debt is, in essence, right and perfect since it frees you from that debt and lightens your karmic load, no matter how uncomfortable paying back the debt may be.

MEDITATION

SCIENCE STATES THAT man is made of energy. Science also states that energy cannot be destroyed, it simply takes another form. This being the case, then you are a walking, talking, living, breathing creature of energy and, as you already know, energy is incredibly versatile and flexible. Learning to control the energy flow in your body and understanding its effects on you and your surroundings can play an enormous role in helping you to keep balanced and healthy. When you become in control of your own energy flow, you become empowered.

Your body has within it many energy vortexes. These are power points where energy can flow in and out with more intensity. While there are hundreds of vortexes in your body, you need only to primarily concern yourself with the seven major vortexes when you are working with body maintenance.

Another term for a vortex is a chakra. Although I was introduced to the term vortex by Urla-Ra, chakra is the more common word used in the holistic and metaphysical worlds. Either is acceptable and you may find me shifting back and forth between the two terms in an effort to familiarize you with both so don't let this confuse you.

Each chakra is a different color and has its own influence on your body. (I will discuss color in more depth further in this book) Although you will find several variations for the color of a chakra and its function in accordance to the religious-spiritual sect, I am using the most common perception.

The base of your spine chakra is called the root chakra. The root chakra vibrates to the color red and influences your emotions. (I.E. seeing red when angry or signifying the red heart when feeling love).

Your abdomen is where the second chakra is located. The second chakra vibrates to the color orange and is significant with creativity. [The female reproductive organs are in the second chakra].

The third chakra is in your stomach area. The common name for this chakra is the solar plexus. The solar plexus vibrates to the color yellow. This chakra deals with instincts. You may have heard someone say that they had a "gut feeling" about someone or something. This is the reaction of their solar plexus.

Your fourth chakra is called the heart chakra and is located in just that area. Your heart chakra vibrates to the color green. It is stated in some religions that the heart chakra is the home of the soul. This area deals with healthy emotions, health, and wellbeing.

The fifth chakra is in your throat area, therefore is it also referred to as your throat chakra. Vibrating to the color blue or indigo, it deals with communications. (The throat chakra is often termed the communicative chakra since your vocal chords are in this area).

The sixth chakra is in the middle of your forehead. Commonly called the third eye, this chakra vibrates to the color of purple or violet. The

third eye chakra can provide visions for the seeker.

At the top or crown of your head is the

seventh chakra. This is, naturally called the crown chakra and vibrates to the color gold or a glowing white. (Often depicted as halo's in paintings of saints) Because of the high vibration of the fifth, sixth and seventh chakras, they are often perceived in varied shades by individuals. For example: Your throat chakra may be perceived as blue to some and indigo to others. Your third eye is often perceived as purple, but some may see it as violet while your crown chakra is reported as glowing white by most but can also be depicted as gold.

Your crown chakra is connected to the Divine and is the main avenue that Divine energy uses when entering your body. The vibration of the crown chakra has been depicted through history as a halo around a person's head.

In order for your body to be perfectly balanced, the energy of these vortexes (chakras) must be spinning in unison in the same direction, which is normally clockwise. (Since we are all individuals, I have met people who have spun counterclockwise. Don't be alarmed if that is the case with you) When you are stressed or ill, you are sure to find that your chakras are not spinning in the same direction or in unison (at the same rate of speed). When you are balancing your chakras, as when you are manifesting through prayer or other means, you will be using thought or speech or writing, or all three.

To balance your chakras, you must begin by visualizing your body in your mind. This can be done either by actually seeing it before you or sensing it as you are housed within it. Either way is acceptable. A chakra balancing guidance tape allows someone else to walk you through the exercise.

It is important to remember that we are all individuals and what works well for one person may not work as well for another. Find what "fits' you and go with it.

Here is a visualization exercise for balancing your chakras. It can be done daily or whenever you feel it is needed. Please note that your energy spins through your body in an upward motion, like a funnel. Start with a clockwise direction, but if it feels extremely "wrong" then switch to a counterclockwise direction.

Begin by visualizing your base chakra (vortex) as a large disc projecting flat out from your body (similar to a hoola-hoop) and it is the color red. Begin spinning this disc in a clockwise direction. As the rate of speed picks up and intensifies, allow any excess red energy to fly off in the form of tiny pellets (like little raindrops) into the universe so that they can be stored and transmuted into positive energy that can be used by yourself or someone else in the future. Do this until you are no longer able to visualize pellets being released from the disc.

Now, go to the second chakra (vortex) which is in the abdomen. Visualize an orange disc like you did with the red disc and begin spinning it. As the chakra begins to spin in a clockwise direction, allow tiny pellets of excess orange energy to release into the universe. When the speed of the orange chakra is compatible with the speed of the red chakra, allow these edges to meld together to create one spinning chakra that is red and orange.

When you are no longer able to visualize orange pellets being released from the disc, begin to spin the yellow chakra in the same manner. When the speed of the yellow chakra becomes compatible with the speed of the orange-red chakra, allow the edges to meld together and create one yellow-orange-red chakra. When you are no longer able to visualize tiny pellets of excess yellow energy being released into the universe, move up the heart chakra and begin spinning the green disc in a clockwise manner. When the speed of the green disc has become compatible with the speed of the yellow-orange-red disc, allow the edges to meld together and create a green-yellow-orange-red chakra disc.

Continue to focus on the green chakra until you can no longer see any more tiny pellets of excess green energy being released into the universe, then move up to the throat chakra. Spin the blue disc in a clockwise manner and when the speed of the blue disc is compatible with the speed of the green-yellow-orange-red disc, allow the edges to meld together to create on blue-green-yellow-orange-red chakra disc. Continue the spinning until you are unable to visualize any more tiny blue pellets of blue energy being released into the universe and then move up to the third eye area and begin spinning the purple disc. Allow the tiny pellets of excess purple energy to be released into the universe as the speed of the purple disc catches up to the speed of the blue-green-yellow-orange-red disc. (Which now resembles a cylinder

around your body).

When you are unable to visualize any more pellets of excess purple energy being released into the universe go up to the crown of your head. The crown chakra is a brilliant white. Begin spinning the white disc in a clockwise direction while you allow any excess pellets of white energy to be released into the universe. When the speed of the white disc is compatible with the speed of the purple-blue-green-yellow-orange-red disc, allow the edges to meld together. Continue focusing on the spinning until you can no longer visualize any excess white energy being released into the universe.

Now, visualize a beam of bright white light coming down from the heavens. Allow this beam of light to enter through the top of your head and go right down the center of the cylinder (discs) that has been formed by melding the edges of your chakras together as they continue to spin. See the beam of light come out of the bottom of the cylinder and into the ground. You are now perfectly balanced and connected to heaven and earth.

NOTE: Many people do not have the ability to visualize as easily as they can just sense or know. If you are unable to visualize, that is fine. Remember, you are an individual. Simply know; experience and feel.

Although meditation is primarily associated with spirituality and metaphysics, let's focus on the physical and scientific aspect of it for a moment.

Everything considered matter, whether you can see it or not, is made up of atoms or pure energy. Therefore, everything is energy in motion and the energy is controlled by thought. Think about that! The consciousness of a person is actually a transmitter of energy, directing the forces that destroy or create form and experience. [We ARE co-creators with Infinite Creator]

There is power in thought, there is power in speech, and there is power in the written word. Through meditation, creative visualization, and the spoken and written word, you can alter the force of energy.

Scientific studies have determined that meditation affects your body. While you are in meditation, the electrical activity of your brain synchronizes and brings balance and harmony to brain waves that have been out of phase and on different frequencies. The result is a higher level of intelligence and creativity. Meditation also normalizes your nervous system and causes many physiological changes that are of great benefit to your physical system.

Meditation is the state of mind and body relaxation that allows you to key into your inner-self, connect with your spiritual guides, and instruct your body on its course to wellness. There are several types of meditation being practiced in the world that I am aware of, and I am sure more that I am not.

It is my understanding that in earlier times meditation was one of the tools used in magical ceremonies. This would make sense, since coming in tune with your own connection with divine energies is necessary in any type of manifestation. An example would be a tribal healer, commonly called the shaman, meditated when asking for any

guidance or assistance from the spirit world.

Today, meditation is used to enhance spiritual growth and enlightenment in most of the world religions. This includes Christianity, Judaism, and Islam. Although you will find it more commonly practiced in the Far East rather than in the West, meditation has been catching on more recently as a recognized tool for stress management.

The majority of Asian traditions emphasize techniques of mental control, similar to some of the newer approaches to psychotherapy. Artists and poets have been known to use meditation as a way to open their minds and allow inspiration to flow.

Stress relief is within the wide range of benefits that can be obtained through meditation. Its effects on your physical body have been documented by science to the degree that it is now a part of the required studies of some medical universities in the United States. The mechanics of how the changes that take place in your body are produced is not completely understood by science, but it was determined clearly that meditation can be used to help relieve stress and ease your body's tension.

It has also been determined that when certain people are under stress, they release a cortisol hormone in their body that actually manufactures and promotes fat. That is why some people gain weight when they are upset, even if they have not increased their food intake. These people, in particular, would benefit from a daily practice of meditation. An easy to spot symptom of excessive cortisol in your body (other than weight gain) would be a fatty paunch or hump at the base of your neck and upper back and puffy cheeks.

Scientists recorded brain wave patterns during meditation and noted they differ from brain wave patterns during sleep. This eliminated the misconception that the benefits are received simply by keeping still and not necessarily through meditation.

Some of the reactions observed during meditation are the lowering of oxygen consumption and a slowing of your heart rate. Although it is possible for your blood pressure to lower after just one meditation session, it generally takes a habitual practice before consistent lowering of blood pressure occurs. Doctors who have treated people with mild-hypertension have been known to recommend meditation along with a good exercise program and a healthy diet, rather than prescription drugs.

Another benefit to meditation is the decreasing of acid levels in your blood. High levels of acid in your blood is associated with anxiety.

And of course, there is the emotional side of life. Some psychotherapists utilize meditation when helping patients cope with or even overcome emotional issues.

There are many types of meditation. I encourage you to explore and experiment with as many as you can in order to find which is most suited for you. One of the more favored forms of meditation is **Transcendental Meditation** or TM. TM became prominent in the USA in the 1960's when it was made popular by many celebrities such as the Beatles. The founder of TM is Maharishi Mahesh Yogi, who studied physics in his native country of India before he began his studies of meditation. TM is relatively easy to learn and generally only requires a few sessions with an instructor to understand it and be able to do it on your own. The main feature of TM is the chanting of the mantra. A mantra is usually a single syllable such as "OM." (The Christian translation for "OM" is "The Word")

Another type of meditation is **Motion Meditation**. When doing Motion Meditation, you actually keep your body in motion while you focus on a specific thought, such as the word "peace." This is a common type of meditation for those who have a lot of excess energy and a difficult time allowing themselves to relax long enough for their body to sink into another form of meditation. Motion Meditation is a part of the practice of Tai Chi. You can find some form of Motion Meditation being practiced in most Buddhist temples.

Guided Meditation allows you to relax and imagine yourself in your favorite spot, plus you have the extra benefit of having someone else lead you while you simply follow his or her suggestions. This immediately places you in a relaxed state because you do not have to do anything more than just follow and respond to the suggestions. Guided Meditation is thought to be a very therapeutic process and I highly recommend it for the beginner.

The form of meditation I teach is **Receptive**

Meditation. Although all are good, this method of meditation was taught to me by Urla-Ra and is used to assist with the proper development of channels throughout your body. You do not train your mind to remain still. The intent here is to just continue to allow the information and energy to flow in and then release it. You need to trust that amongst the "monkey chatter" the desired and needed information is flowing in and know that whatever should stay, will stay and whatever should go, will go. By doing this, you are fine tuning your body to the universal energies that it will channel. Receptive Meditative follows the concept of the Universal Law of Abundance. You focus less on control and more on simply performing the necessary steps. Have faith and allow things to flow. You will begin to receive and channel more and more of the universal energies.

Because you are seeking a clear avenue for the energies to flow in Receptive Meditation, you should never cross your arms or legs. You can sit with your legs stretched before you or with your feet flat on the floor. Or you may lie down. (Be careful when you lie down that you don't go to sleep) I suggest to my students that they think of a water hose. The idea is to keep the kinks out of it so that the water (energy) can flow freely through it. To quote Urla-Ra, "When this occurs, that which should remain with you in the form of information or healing energy will indeed remain with you. That which should continue on, will flow out and back into the universe."

When you are in a receptive meditative state, you are giving up control Therefore it is important for you to first surround yourself with protection. The following is a wonderful invocation to do just that:

"I call upon the universal energies. I call upon the highest of the high to surround me and enfold me and embrace me in the golden protective light of the universe. I invoke the Archangels... Gabriel, Rafael, Uriel, and Michael and ask that they form a clear and protective avenue of communication between myself and the divine."

You may, at this time, invoke the presence of your own spirit guide(s) if you wish.

After doing this invocation, you can state an insight that you are seeking (such as clarity on a specific situation) or a result that you are seeking (such as peace and relaxation) and allow your body to relax and receive.

A good length for a meditation session is twenty minutes, but you are not locked into that time frame. I have been known to meditate for as little as five minutes or for as long as eight hours.

You possess, within you, the ability to accomplish everything that may you set out to accomplish. When you discover, through meditation, how to be in harmony with Infinite Creator and Infinite Creator's creative energies, you are experiencing a privilege and a blessing that so many are not aware of. Through meditation, you can obtain the guidance of wisdom and inner realization that can head off avoidable difficulty and unhappiness; which inevitably lead to stress.

I suggest that you keep a journal of your meditation sessions. When you write down the thoughts that you remember or the experiences that you have had while in meditation and look them over at least once a month, you will be surprised at the clarity they can bring to your life. And of course, if you have clarity of a situation you can deal with it more comfortably, thus relieving or eliminating a stressor in your life.

MANIFESTING SUCCESS

"YOU CREATE YOUR OWN reality."

This popular statement suggests that your success in life is of your own creation. Why is it then that some people are extremely successful while others are still struggling? I feel there are a variety of reasons.

Through the energy of thought and belief, you can accept or reject certain vibrations in your environment. Therefore, your success in life does not only depend upon your ability and training, it also depends upon your beliefs and your determinations to use all of the abilities and gifts that have been given to you by Infinite Creator and how you grasp at the opportunities when they are presented.

If you use all the available outward means, as

well as your own natural abilities to overcome every

obstacle in your path, you will be using the gifts that Infinite Creator has given you. These gifts are unlimited with their usage and flow from your innermost being. Of these gifts, there are two very important ones. They are thought and free-will.

Did you know that you demonstrate success or failure every day in your thinking? What is your strongest thinking pattern; the one that you are investing the most emotion into? Are your thoughts of success or of failure? Are they filled with joy and anticipation or fear and dread?

It is so easy to fall into a negative thought pattern without even realizing it, especially if you are surrounded by stressful negatives in your actions and words. Do you find yourself engaging with others in negative conversations throughout the day? What are the primary words you use in a sentence? Are they positive or negative? Remember that you are responsible for your own thoughts. So, what are you thinking?

Here is some food for thought:

When you are constantly placing a problem

under mental review, you are prohibiting it from working itself out. I equate that to writing a letter but not releasing it into the mail system. It is important for you to stay positive and detached and know, "It is as it should be." That does not mean that you should bury your head and do nothing. There is an old Arab saying; "Trust in Infinite Creator but tie your camel!"

So, what does it mean? It means to relax, be still, have faith that all is in right and perfect order for you at this time, then do the necessary steps to allow the energies to flow in a manner that will provide the path for a right and perfect solution. If you attune with your inner being, commune with Infinite Creator, and connect with your spiritual guides for assistance through prayer or meditation, you will be able to think correctly regarding everything you do and the correct channels for rectifying a situation will be placed before you. I know that this seems easier said than done. But, with time and practice it will become like second nature. When you feel your thoughts or notice your actions becoming negative, rather than expend the energy on worrying about this or that, why not expend that same energy training yourself to NOT worry about it? It does not have to be an elaborate process, as long as it is comfortable for you and it works. My favorite statement when I catch myself in a negative thought pattern is a simple "cancel, cancel!" Conscious practice and effort will inevitably replace any habit and if you stick to it, it will eventually seem effortless. In my hypnotic studies I learned that, without hypnosis to help shift a pattern, the normal time frame for developing a new habit is twenty days. Let's face it. Every day of your life you are using will-power in some way to maintain or develop a habit. Whether this habit is a positive one or a negative one is up to you. But, if you are expending the energy anyway (whether consciously or unconsciously) doesn't it make sense to create a positive habit? Practice on a conscious level and the sub-conscious will follow.

Every outward manifestation is the result of your use of your own will. Your conscious mind uses a force that is accompanied by determination and effort. Since, as you retrain your conscious mind, your subconscious mind will follow, it is important to select your use of conscious free-will carefully. Take the time to think about what you are manifesting and make certain that it is for your highest good. If you are uncertain in any way, I recommend that you go into meditation and ask Infinite Creator, your higher self, or your guides for guidance in the matter. If you still feel it is right and perfect for you, then proceed with the manifestation.

Here is a powerful statement. "Your mind is the creator of all experiences." Wow! Think about that. We are all co-creators with Infinite Creator. Everything comes from Infinite Creator; that is true. So yes, Infinite Creator creates all. But you have been given free-will to choose how and what is created. Isn't that an amazing concept, and a tricky one? Are you choosing to allow only the good in your life?

I am sure you have heard the saying "Be careful what you ask for, you just might get it." Did you know that if you cling to a certain thought with enough emotion behind it, it will eventually take a tangible outward form? The creative energies of the Universe cannot discern between a stressful thought and a non-stressful thought; therefore, it will bring forth the strongest and most consistent thought. Think of poverty all the time and remain in poverty, think of abundance all of the time, and watch abundance manifest in your life. Can you see now how, in many ways, you do indeed control your own destiny?

Remember that we humans are the ones who have created lack. Infinite Creator knows only abundance. If you keep yourself in communion with Infinite Creator and the abundance that is available to you, there can be no lack in your life. Prosperity, success, and abundance in all areas of your life are yours by divine right. Allow them to flow to you! It is really okay. If you recall the teachings of the bible, the great Master Jesus did just such a thing on numerous occasions. Master Jesus also stated, "That which I do, so can ye do."

You are a storehouse of life energy and this energy is constantly working your bodily functions as well as your thoughts. So, if you have fear, it is an emotion that will exhaust some of your life energy that is flowing through your mind. You read earlier about how fear creates a tremendous amount of stress on your body (the fight or flight syndrome). If you keep your consciousness focused in positive thoughts that are in unison with the universe, fear absolutely can't survive. Combine your positive thoughts with courage, faith and proper body maintenance and you have the key to reducing, overcoming and or eliminating any stressor.

Do you understand the difference between intent and a wish? This is an important factor when manifesting. Wishes are wonderful but accomplish very little. If you are making a wish, you desire without the necessary energy to back it up. After a wish it is important to exercise intention by following through with the action of doing. In other words, in order to fulfill a wish or a desire, you need to act upon the wish. Your "act" should be allowing yourself to commune with Infinite Creator with the purest of heart's intent. It is then that you release the true power of life's energy. This cannot happen by merely wishing passively and hoping for a miracle to make your wishes to become reality.

Now, let's address the topic of failure. What if you fail? So... what if you do fail? I strongly encourage you to never allow failure to become a stressor, because it is simply a learning process. Try your best to keep this in mind and allow it to be the driving force that pushes you closer toward achieving your goal(s). If you fail at manifesting your desire and you are sure your desire is right and perfect for you, I suggest you analyze each factor in the situation in order to discover where you erred and eliminate all chances of repeating the same errors in the future. I feel that a good way to cope with and overcome the concept of failure is to read about all of the many successful people in the world who experienced their own learning processes (failures) prior to recognizing their goals. Bookstores and libraries are full of just such stories.

Increased focus of your attention, combined with a good plan, trust, and directed energy are signs of positive growth after any kind of failure. It is easy to fall into the trap of stressful impatience and quit too soon. You can avoid this if you keep in mind that the universe has its own time clock that doesn't always match your own. Patience and persistence are vital when you are manifesting, as well as faith and trust. You have heard the saying "As fate would have it," correct? Well, to that I say, "There is no such thing as fate." Not of that nature anyway. We create our own fate by our actions or our in-actions. Success and failure are simply the results of what you have done in the past and what you are doing in the present. This is why it is so important to review your successes and recreate those thoughts. Enhance them until they are able to overrule the influence of any negative tendencies of your past, in this life or another.

If you want success, it is necessary that you reject all thoughts of failure. Transmute any negative thoughts into positive and successful ones as soon as they appear. Use the methods described in this book, or something of your own that you are comfortable with, to help you convert anxiety into tranquility. Another important factor is to focus on your desire with minimal mental or emotional distractions. As your stress eases and you experience peacefulness, you can connect with the Divine connection that resides within you. This state of self-realization is a valuable tool for manifesting your goals so that you can enjoy, more fully, your journey through life.

Another tool to help manifest your desires is self-analysis. This does not mean self-criticism. Analysis and criticism are not the same. Self-analysis is a way in which you can see into the recesses of your mind and discover aspects of your shadow-self that might otherwise remain hidden. Through self-analysis, you can sort out your positive and negative tendencies and discover what might be blocking you. I would like to clarify that analyzing does not mean dwelling on something. Analyzing is a constructive and abstract way of looking at a situation or emotion. When you take the time to determine the nature of your mission in life, it will be easier for you to manifest whatever you desire, thus creating a stress-less environment. Of course, your ultimate purpose is to experience life and grow spiritually, but you also have tasks to perform while you are experiencing life. Your degree of success in performing these tasks will determine how you will increase in your spiritual growth.

It is very difficult to see the value in a life lesson when you are overcome by stress. Staying focused, with minimal stress, while combining energy with initiative, will help you to recognize and appreciate those wonderful lessons of life and enjoy the achievements of your goals.

Many people excuse their own faults while

judging others quite harshly. What if they excused

other people for what they believe to be a shortcoming and simply focused on themselves? Although it may be necessary to analyze others at times, I suggest that you keep your mind unprejudiced. If you can learn to see Infinite Creator in all people of whatever race or creed, you will truly know what Divine Love is. Feeling your connection with every human being and forgetting your individual-self while you glimpse at your Infinite Creator-self, the Spirit that unifies all men. You will find your life more fulfilled with less stress and more pleasure. As I stated earlier, a truly spiritual person does not focus on or judge another for their faults or flaws; but instead they focus on themselves with the intent of improvement.

It is important to remember that your habits will either hinder or assist your growth rate. It is not your fleeting thoughts as much as it is your everyday mental habits that control your life's progression. Your habits of consistent thoughts are mental habits that control your life's progression. Remember, you create your own reality. Your consistent thoughts are magnets that draw to you certain things, people, and conditions. If you make a habit of positive thoughts, you will attract benefits and opportunities, while negative thoughts will attract you to unhappy and undesirable persons, environments, and situations.

As I mentioned earlier, I simply say the words "cancel, cancel" when I find myself dwelling on a thought process that is not positive. If you feel that is not enough, you can also avoid things, situations and/or people that prompt any focus to a negative thought or feeling. I think it is important to point out that by avoiding a person who promotes a negative habit in you, you are not necessarily judging them. You are simply recognizing the negative impact they have on you. He or she may be a wonderful person who would be a perfect companion for someone else, but just not right for you at this time.

When you decline to keep the company of any individual whom you have determined, through analysis of a situation, is promoting a negative pattern within you, you are exercising self-love, not judgment of others. It is not always an easy thing to do, since there may be times when his or her feelings are hurt and, of course, for most people the concept of hurting someone else's feelings is quite stressful. Do your best to find a way to release yourself from the situation as gracefully as possible and remember that you really can't hurt someone's feelings unless they react to the situation in a manner that allows them to feel hurt. Once you have determined what needs to be avoided, be it a person or a thing, then work on diverting your mind and visualize yourself doing a more positive thing or with a person(s) more suitable to your needs and move toward it/them; patience and persistence may be something you will have to exercise. Since it takes about twenty days to develop a new habit, it stands to reason it would take equally as long to alter and release an old habit. If you would like to speed up that process, then I recommend the assistance of hypnosis.

Everyone has within them a direct connection with Infinite Creator. This connection gives you the power to create or manifest. The accomplishments of someone who uses this creative tool at optimum, in my opinion, are nothing short of profound. Just think about it. By manifesting something from nothing, you are demonstrating that the seemingly impossible is possible! All you have done is align with the universal flow of energies and use those marvelous

Infinite Creator given abilities that you possess within you. When you truly understand the concept and methods for manifesting in your life, you will realize freedom, prosperity, good health, happiness, joy, and stress-less living to the fullest extent.

One of the most vital secrets to true freedom is the practice of self-control. I believe that until you are truly able to command yourself to do the things you know you should do, (but may not want to do) you are not in charge of your life. In that power of self-control, is eternal freedom. In that power of self-control is the foundation of manifestation.

The great Master Jesus said: "Thy will be done."

When you attune your will to Infinite Creator's will, you are using Divine Will. Through the use of the right techniques, along with meditation, you can achieve perfect harmony with the Universe. This is

what brings to fruition desired manifestations.

All power lies in your connection to the will of

Infinite Creator and all spiritual and material gifts flow from Infinite Creator's boundless abundance. In order to receive Divine gifts, you need to release from your mind any thoughts of limitation and poverty. Remember, Infinite Creator knows no limitations. This is in all aspects of your life, not just financial.

Since Infinite Creator is perfect and knows no lack and you are made in the image of Infinite Creator and have a direct line to Infinite Creator's manifestation gifts, to reach the limitless universal supply that Infinite Creator has provided, it is important for you to maintain a consciousness of abundance. Even when you don't know where your next dollar is coming from, the best manifestation is done without fear or doubt. I know it sounds easier said than done, but with time and practice it will become second nature. When you become proficient in this, you won't fear where your next dollar is coming from. You will just trust that you are doing your part, and everything is in right and perfect order.

When you find yourself starting to become

irritated or impatient with a person or a situation,

do your best to relax and work through it. When you do your part and rely on the energies to follow, you will find the Universal Forces coming to your aid and your constructive thoughts will materialize, no matter what your desired outcome. Keep in mind that your confidence in manifestation, connection to the Divine, and consciousness of abundance and balance become intensified through meditation.

Since Infinite Creator is the source of all, including peace and prosperity, when you are preparing to manifest, the first step would be to make connection with Infinite Creator's divine energy. By doing this, you are creating a clear channel to use your abilities and other universal energies to achieve maximum results. Just as you cannot broadcast through a broken transmitter, it is also true with prayers and manifestations. You cannot send out effective prayers or affirmations through your body's transmitter that has been off balanced by restlessness and negativity. By becoming peaceful within yourself and focusing on positive thinking, you can repair your mind's ability to transmit clearly and increase the receptivity of your intuition. This means you will be able to broadcast to the universe effectively and receive your answers and results more clearly.

The majority of the balanced men and women, that I am aware of, spend a good deal of their time in concentration. They are able to dive deeply within their minds and find the right and perfect solutions for the problems confronting them. These people withdraw their attention from all distractions while they focus. The have developed a habit. Unfortunately, many of them, I have noticed, also use this habit for manifesting success in material aspects only and neglect their health, spiritual or emotional needs. Remember, success and abundance are not measured strictly by material means. You can't call yourself truly balanced unless you have reached a state of "I'm okay, you're okay" in all areas of your life. The focus is to live a stress-less life, which means all aspects of your life, not just the monetary, need to be in balance. When you are manifesting through prayer, you will be using thought, speech, writing or even all three. Remember, there is power in thought, power in

speech and power in the written word.

As I stated earlier, your body is a storehouse

of energy. Energy is constantly being used in muscular movements such as the functioning of your heart, lungs, and diaphragm; in cellular metabolism and chemicalization of the blood and in carrying on the functions of your nervous system. Besides this, a tremendous amount of energy goes into thought and emotion. Fear and confusion are two of the greatest opposites of the dynamic faith and ambition and can deplete your life energy flow. (Also known as "life force") They cause the life force, which would ordinarily flow steadily through your nerves themselves, to become almost paralyzed. (fight or flight syndrome).

The vitality in your entire body lessens.

Fear and confusion don't help you get away from a situation. Instead, they weaken your sense of commitment, desire, and drive. They will constrict your heart, both physically and emotionally, interfere with the function of your digestive system, and help create many other physical disturbances of which I covered in the beginning of this book. When your consciousness is kept positive and you have no fears or confusions, courage and faith come into play and provide you

with a comfortable and stress-less lifestyle.

Now, let's revisit the concept of wishing for something vs. manifesting something. If you make a wish, you are having a desire without energy. After a wish, you might go through the motions of a plan to fulfill your wish or desire, but in order to assure the results are what you are looking for you must act until you get your wish. When you do this, the life force is released in a steady stream that will promise results. When you merely wish passively to be able to obtain and objective and make a feeble and half-hearted effort to achieve it without communing with Divine universal energies, the odds are very strong that you will accomplish nothing.

These efforts should be well planned and charged with increased and deliberate attention. I can't emphasize enough how important I believe it is not to give in to the temptation of accepting failure as fate. Whether you are experiencing success or failure, these are the direct or indirect results of what you have done in the past and what you are doing now. So, when you feel you have failed, pick yourself up, dust yourself off and recall all of the successful thoughts of your past. Analyze what you did vs. what you could have done. Do adequate researches in the area of your goal and incorporate prayer and meditation and remember to be positive and relaxed.

One of the strongest attributes of successful person, in my opinion, is the fact that the person has trained himself/herself to reject the thought of failure. He or she learns to transfer any thoughts of failure into just the opposite. Anxiety is converted into tranquility through the use of will. He or she takes control of a restless mind and harnesses it while he or she connects with the divine powers within. I feel very strongly that when you attain this state of self-realization, you can truly enjoy your life more fully. And when you are happy and enjoying your life, you are no longer a victim of stress.

You will notice that I stated successful people train themselves to shift their negative thoughts into positive thoughts. So many people are under the misconception that just because they have decided to be positive, there is no work involved in maintaining it. Would that such a thing be true! I admit that it gets easier over time to develop the habit of being positive, but most of the people I know, myself included, have good days and bad days. During those good days, yes, it is very easy to be up-beat and positive. It is those down days that require some initiative and use of willpower to keep on track. No matter how developed you are in your knowledge of spirituality and using willpower to correct the fact that you are having a down day, there is no shame if you find yourself experiencing one. Some of the greatest success stories are a result of an initial down day that required a person to get quiet, get relaxed and get in alignment with Infinite Creator's universal flow. I like to call this universal flow "the river of life."

Because you are an individual, you have the ability to create something that no one else has ever created. You do things in new ways by using your desire and willpower. Just look at the accomplishments recorded about people displaying this throughout history. By what appears to be creating something from nothing, you are demonstrating that the seemingly impossible can become possible by employing your connections with Infinite Creator's creative energies that are always

at your disposal.

Creating things that make your life easier and more enjoyable is only one of the many ways to release stress from your life. Compatibility with your fellow man is equally important. This is where it becomes necessary to release your tendencies to be judgmental or excessively critical. By seeing Infinite Creator in all of man-kind your odds of developing patience and understanding will increase, and your stress level will decrease.

If you are able to free yourself from negative habits and you are able to do good because you want to do it and not merely because you feel you have to do it.

When you reach the point where you are doing this automatically, I think that is a good indication that you have truly progressed in spirit. When you feel progressed in spirit, it brings about a sensation of satisfaction and balance that will help eliminate stress in your life. It's a domino effect.

I have encountered, on various occasions, the popular Eastern philosophy: "The things you need in life are those that will help to fulfill your dominant purpose. The things you may want but not need may lead you aside from that purpose. It is only by making everything serve your main purpose that success is attained."

No truer words were ever spoken. Achieving goals that are not in your highest good can only bring on stress in the end. As I have stated earlier, you should think about whether fulfillment of a particular goal you have chosen will provide success for you. Before you can do that, we need to analyze what success is.

So, what is success and why is it so important?

I am covering success in such depth because, as I stated earlier, you are not balanced if you are not successful in all areas of your life. Of course, success is measured differently by people. My perception of success is when you have balance in all aspects of your life. If you possess health and wealth but have trouble with everybody (including yourself) is your life a successful life? Is success really success if you aren't experiencing happiness?

Success can't be measured by the worldly standard of wealth and prestige and power, since none of these are guaranteed to provide true happiness if they are not used correctly. You will know if you are using them correctly if you are experiencing a sense of fulfillment, happiness, peace, and harmony within yourself. If you are not experiencing these things, after achieving your goal(s), then, I would suggest you reevaluate your goals!

Here is a concept that may be difficult to understand at first. Infinite Creator does not punish you; nor does Infinite Creator reward you. Not in the sense that most religions instill into their congregation, anyway. What Infinite Creator does do is give you the power to reward or punish yourself through the use or misuse of your own reason, will and creative usage of His universal laws. If you transgress the laws of health, prosperity, and wisdom, you will suffer from sickness, poverty, or ignorance. However, this can be altered if you shift your thought process and refuse to allow negativity, false beliefs, and detrimental actions to remain in your reality. Your happiness depends, to some extent, upon external conditions; but chiefly upon your mental attitudes. Stress levels vary with each individual. What might be considered stressful to one person could make another person perfectly content. There are a few general guidelines for humanity that I have deduced through my interactions and associations with my fellow man over the years as well as my own thoughts.

They are as follows: Good health, a well-balanced mind; an abundant life; the right employment of your energies; a thankful attitude in your heart; love of your fellow man, beast, and the planet earth; and a workable understanding and knowledge of the gifts that have been bestowed upon you for your use.

If you follow these guidelines and select your goals in accordance to them, I feel confident that you will experience a reduced stress level in your life, as well as many other wonderful things.

Simply stated, if you allow yourself to pour forth, in a constructive manner, the positive thoughts, beliefs and abilities that you already have, more will come. It is the Law! When you do your absolute best to align yourself with Infinite Creator's creative energy flow, you will be in contact with the Divine Power that will help you solve any problem that arises, as well as create fantastic new possibilities for your life experience. Power from this wonderful communion with Infinite Creator will flow uninterruptedly and you will be able to use your inherent creativity in any sphere of activity; bringing success, harmony, and balance and best of all- reduced stress!

I suggest that, when you are making major decisions, you sit in silence and ask for the guidance that is always available to you. Tap into the power of Infinite Creator that is behind you at all times. Behind your mind, is Infinite Creator's mind; behind your will is Infinite Creator's will. Since Infinite Creator knows no failure, when Infinite Creator is working with you it is impossible to fail. Although your answers can and do come directly from Infinite Creator, many religious upbringing and programming prohibit people from comfortably communicating directly with Infinite Creator and feeling worthy of a direct response. If this is the case with you, your spirit guides are happy to assist as the "go between." Just "Ask and ye shall receive." When it is done with purity of heart's intent, it happens every time. There are twelve laws by which the universe is directed. It is important that you recognize and understand these laws prior to your manifestation work. By understanding these laws and utilizing them correctly, you will receive the desired response for your efforts. These laws are as follows.

1] **Natural Law**:

The law that Infinite Creator set in motion to govern all creation. It is mutable and unchangeable. I am aware of no instance where Infinite Creator set aside this law in response to human appeal or for any other reason.

2] **Law of Life**:

The law that controls the relationship of Infinite Creator and living things; our ability to adjust ourselves to it determines the power of Infinite Creator that is expressed through us.

3] **Law of Love**:

The creative force of all life, it is the highest
vibration that can be attained; for love is Infinite
Creator and Infinite Creator is love.

4] **Law of Truth**:

The knowledge which constitutes right thinking, right action, and right living; truth will always rise triumphant over evil and wrong-doing. Truth leads us onward toward a better and higher understanding of life.

5] **Law of Compensation**:

The law which provides you with just payment for your own acts, whether good or bad; the law of compensation automatically exacts its punishment or reward (karma).

6] **Law of Freedom**:

The law that teaches you your unlimited power of choice; you can live as you desire, suffering or progressing, in accordance with those desires.

7] **Law of Vibration**:

The law that teaches us that all things in the
universe are vibrating and their rate of vibration determines their nature and expression.

8] **Law of Attraction**:

The law that may be considered the drawing force in the universe that causes creations to be attracted to each other.

9] **Law of Evolution**:

The law that guarantees progression of life; each individual expression is creating a higher state of consciousness for itself. What may appear regression is simply a mis-understanding regarding the law of evolution. This law deals with the effects of each state of consciousness on the individualized life and not on its outward manifestation. It affords us comforting knowledge that all life will eventually arrive at conscious atonement (at-one-ment) with Infinite Creator, the Creator.

10] **Law of Mind**:

The higher mind has authority over the lower mind that gives form and manifestation to all matter. Through focus and concentration, the lower mind is brought into rapport with the higher mind and obeys its design. The higher mind can and does control the minds of its environment.

11] **Law of Transmutation**:

The law that states that all manifestations, both physical and ethereal, are of the same basic substance known to the scientist as energy but referred to by the spiritual-holistic-meta-physical world as Spirit. The rate of vibration determines the outward manifestation of Spirit. Change the rate of vibration and the manifestation changes as well.

12] **Law of Abundance**:

The law based on your ability to live in the consciousness of your at-one-ment with Infinite Creator. It expresses as you reflect this consciousness in your own life, for the law of abundance is Infinite Creator's heritage to His children.

As you recognize who you are and accept this knowledge the law of abundance manifests in your

life.

AFFIRMATIONS

"CONTROLLED THOUGHT results in the control of what you experience."
Unknown

Since your thoughts determine, to a large degree, the functioning and health of your physical body, your relationships with others and success in achieving your goal(s), it would make sense that if you developed a method of discipline and carefully watched what enters into your thoughts, you will be able to program yourself to commune more fully with Infinite Creator, thus work with the universal laws more effectively. Selecting specific types of thoughts for certain specific results will enable you to enjoy a richer, more fulfilling, stress-less life.

The following is an exercise that will help you to learn to take control of your thought process. Try it for a full seven days. You may find it cannot only be fun, but very productive. While you are doing this exercise, you will probably find that some of the ideas I've written seem new and possibly foreign. Keep in mind that although foreign to you, they are ideas that have been proven over and over again to lead to results at some point and time, through a variety of groups from various walks of life.

It is best if you write down the goals you are looking to achieve before you begin this exercise. Then, when you have completed the exercise, you can see how far you have come and if you are still seeking to accomplish the same goals.

It is very important for you to establish a program of discipline for yourself.

This is where your willpower comes into play. You will need to set aside approximately 15 minutes each day for this exercise. I suggest that you select a time when you are the most receptive and alert. It goes without saying that the results you will see depends upon the sincerity of your efforts.

Day One:

Stay quiet for a moment and think only about yourself. (This is something that most people rarely do as they deal with the stresses of daily living.) Do you remember what you saw when looked in the mirror this morning? You saw a body that was you.

Did you realize that your body is composed of water and a small percentage of chemicals? Along with that, you have emotions, you get hungry, you get cold and you get hot. You have feelings of life, hate, anger, anxiety, fear, and joy. But are these senses and emotions the real you; or is the real you simply experiencing them? Is that what you would say you are? Or would you say you are so much more? If so, then what are you?

Take your time and think about it.

Although your brain is the part of your body where thought resides or passes through, science has been unable to prove that a brain is able to think by itself. With its billions of interconnecting nerves, your brain appears as a type of marvelous computing machine. Grant it, computers are fast and accurate, but they don't think. Your brain, like the computer, is really just a type of machine. Neither one is able to write or create or think on its own. But, you are able to think. You have a body and you are able to feel emotions and senses. You are aware of yourself through the process of thought. You have a life force

flowing through you.

This life force is your Spirit.

Now that you recognize yourself as something with a Spirit, a life force that thinks, the question of where you came from now arises. Are you the water and chemicals that formulate your body? Or, are you a combination of mind, spirit, and body; and if so, where did you come from? What are you really? What you are is an extension of Infinite Creator. You are an individual extension of the expression of Infinite Creator. Everything about you is an individualization of the one great and might Creator.

Affirmation for the day:

I am part of the one great and infinite Creator. Divine energy flows through me and is an expression of all that I am. I decree it; I believe it, and it is so.

Day Two:

Through studies in astronomy we have found that the earth is a relatively small planet that is one of the nine major planets revolving around the sun; which makes it a relatively small star. It is one of the billions located near the edge of a spiral stellar galaxy that you and see on a clear night. Our galaxy is in a universe amongst countless other galaxies. It has been stated that many of the limitless numbers of stars in the universe have planets around them that could possibly have some sort of life on them; and that would make sense. For how pompous can we be to think that we are the only life force in this enormous collection of planets, stars, and galaxies? Your body is made up of the food that you eat, the water that you drink and the air that you breathe. When you think about it, your body is built out of the elements of the planet itself; which, from what science has been able to determine, is made of the same basic elements that make up the sun and even the remotest stars. So, in essence, the materials of which your body is made of and the materials that the stars are made of are basically of the same materials. So, does that make you a part of the universal scheme of things? Absolutely! You are a part of the universe, which is so vast that man has not even begun to comprehend its full nature. You are a part of all that is created. You are a part of it, not separate from it. You are actually a part of all that you can see, and you are just as important as any other part. For you are composed of the same materials as all the other parts. The creative qualities that you possess are also evidence of Infinite Creator's divine intelligence flowing through you and throughout the universe. You are a focal point in an ongoing universal drama. Inherent where you are, are all of the basic materials of the physical universe and all of the intelligence purpose and creative power that exists anywhere. My objective is to make you aware of this and realize that you are part of all that is. As much as you might try, you cannot remove yourself nor isolate yourself from the Divine creative forces.

Now, here is something to contemplate. Infinite Creator's creative forces cannot be in conflict or the universe would be destroyed.

The creative harmony of the universe is available not just in some places, but everywhere. That means where you are as well. The same basic core that all things are made of is surrounding you. This core functions according to the same law and order that holds all of the planets in their places. So, there is basically noting lacking where you are. I repeat. There is nothing lacking where you are.

You have available to you the usage of all that is. When you are able to grasp the full value and meaning of this concept you will be able to grasp how you can use it.

Affirmation for the day:

I have free use of the universal creative laws. There laws are available to everyone. Although there is diversity of use of these laws, the same power which works in me, works in all of mankind. Although I'm a unique individual, I'm not alone. I know that every aspect of my life experience continues to become a more perfect expression and manifestation of the nature of Infinite Creator, which flows through me. And this nature can only be good. I believe it; I decree it and it as so.

Day Three:

Visualize (If you are not good at visualizing,

then simply sense) the size of the planet and also the size of an atom. Notice that in relation to size, you are just about in the middle in the general scope of things. You are neither very big nor very small. When it comes to size, you are really not impressive one way or the other. But, even though you are not impressive in size, in accordance to the scope of things, you are definitely unique. There has never been and there never will be another person or thing exactly like you. Even when people and things might appear similar or alike, there is always a difference that sets them apart. Nature never duplicates itself. Everything is a unique and individual expression of life. Infinite Creator's creative life force is expressing itself in everything. Since there is always a purpose in all life, this means that you have within you a life force that expresses and creates in a manner that will never be duplicated! It is important to remember that your mode of thinking is a particular channel for Infinite Creator's flowing expression.

Life is for living, not for existing. Life holds infinite possibilities for pleasure, happiness, and accomplishment, but only if you allow them. It is important for you to remember that you are the most important person in your world just as every other person is also the most important person in their world. You all take part in the limitless expressions of the one Infinite Creator. No one else can live your life for you and one else can bring into reality Infinite Creator's creativeness the way you can. You are unique. You are important to yourself and to the life force of energy that is flowing through you. You also have an obligation to Infinite Creator to live a good life. Why not meet your potential and assume your responsibility as a co-creator? Only then can you become the best person that you can be. This doesn't mean that you have to become famous or make some profound mark on society. It simply means that you should strive to manifest the things that really count in your life. Whether you remain within your household or reach beyond it, to really be an important self you need to express love, harmony, and creativity for the greatest possible good in all that you do for yourself and for others. In doing this, you will open up the way to be a greater value and importance to yourself and to your fellow man; not to mention the feeling of satisfaction and peace that you will experience from the inside out. Through your efforts in maintaining a positive self-expression, you will bring peace and harmony to your own daily existence and reduce or even eliminate stress. By doing this for yourself, you can also help bring it to others!

Affirmation for the day:

I am an expression of Infinite Creator. Infinite

Creator's creative life force flows through me and is expressing its perfect nature. I am a unique and important individual creation. I decree it; I believe it, and it is so.

Day Four:

Now that you have an idea as to who you are, let's want to focus on your ability to create. It has been established that you are a co-creator with Infinite Creator and have access to the nature of the creative power behind the universe. Your thoughts manifest in accordance with the Universal Laws. Since a thought is energy and actives Divine creation, it stands to reason that it is also creative. Because your thinking determines your experiences, your thoughts become the catalysts for conditions and situations you encounter in daily living. If you are having trouble grasping this concept, don't worry. If it has not already, the time will come when you will have proof and evidence on the validity of this concept. For now, try to accept it at face value and assume that it is true. Just keep at the foremost of your mind that thoughts are energy that can become experiences and the usage of the creative life force through you is a constructive process. It is forever building things up, creating, and organizing in a useful and purposeful manner. This creative life force acts in accordance with the Universal Laws. This being the case, how creative are your thoughts? Are you creating positive experiences or negative experiences in your life with your thought process? We all have free will and you have the divine right to think in whatever manner you desire. It is important for you to realize and understand that the manner in which you are thinking is determining the experiences in your relationship, health, and success. So, how are you thinking? Is your thought pattern enhancing your life or is it costing you?

When you can begin to think in a positive and constructive manner, you will create only good in your life. You will experience obtaining goals rather than just wishing for them. When you have clear, consistent, positive thoughts in your mind, you will have the ability to create only good through your thought process.

Affirmation for the day:

My thoughts are creative energy. The more positive my thoughts, the more powerful my creative abilities for good become. I have within me the ability to create and control in accordance to my thought process. I fill my mind with only positive and constructive thoughts. I know that my entire life is directed by the nature of the thought process that I've chosen. I decree it; I believe it and it is so.

Day Five:

Since you are the one using and manipulating the creative laws, it naturally follows that all the powers of these laws are available to you. They are just there, waiting to come forth in the expression of life that you have selected, in accordance to your thought process. In accordance to the universal law of free will, these infinite possibilities can't force themselves upon you. In order for you to benefit by them, you need to discover and consciously use them. Otherwise, you are basically walking blindly through life.

Your first step is to recognize that they are there. You have only used a small portion of the full capacities you are already recognizing as yours, let alone tapping into the larger resources that are always available. Odds are that you have probably been denying yourself the very things you want most! How?

By letting your thoughts dwell on the things, you do not want rather than on the things you do want. The result is that you have experienced what you dwell on the most. Be they negative or positive, the possibilities that you have in any direction are limitless. It is all in accordance to the use you make of the Universal Laws.

Wouldn't you like to break down the barriers of all limitations and start to use these laws to the fullest? With faith, focus, determined and dedication, the time will come when you will be able to reach down into the bottomless reservoir you have within you and experience the limitless possibilities which are yours simply by your acceptance of them. This is how the greatness of the ages was born. It is how science has discovered and the artist has captured, and the poet has found the depth and meaning of words and the composer has achieved the immortal melodies and the incurable are cured. All have reached down into their well of the possibilities. To a large extent, you are unknowingly using the laws anyway. Remember, just because you are not aware of it, does not mean it does not exist. Universal law has no restrictions or limitations on your thoughts. The laws are non-selective. The limitations placed on your life are the limitations your creative self has placed. Free your pattern of thinking from all thoughts of limitations and realize that the limitless potential of good in the universe is accessible to you. Then you will be able to become the best you can be. Then you will be able to experience to a fuller extent, what is inherent in your life. The creativity and pattern of your thought process is the key to your life experiences

Affirmation for the day:

The Creator knows no limits and neither does his expression through me. I accept the abundant flow of creative energies and I choose to use the Universal Laws to experience a greater self and a stress-free existence. I decree it; I believe it and it is so.

Day Six:

There is no reason for anyone to sit back and complain that the world is let them down or sit back and complain that the world is withheld the things that make living worthwhile. When you acknowledge that the creative life force behind the universe and the Universal Laws are Infinite Creator and with Infinite Creator rests the possibility of all good things, then you will be able to realize that everything is already been made available to you. The challenge is to what degree or extent you are able to recognize and accept this fact.

You are the only one who is withholding yourself from life's abundance. You are able to receive things only to the extent to which you are able to give. When you change your pattern of thinking and concern yourself with what you can contribute to life, you will be surprised at what you will start receiving. The world can supply you with abundant living, but not on the assumption that it is owed to you.

There is a difference between knowing that something is yours by divine right and feeling that it is owed to you. It is necessary for you to become an active participant in life, doing your best to contribute in the best possible manner. "Infinite Creator helps those who help themselves, and each other." I remember listening to a lecture by a famous motivational speaker, who told a story of a man who was given an opportunity to choose whether he wanted to be in heaven or hell. He described hell as a beautiful room filled with a banquet table that contained a feast for kings. It was adorned in the most elaborate settings and had all you would ever need or desire on it. Yet the people at the table were gaunt and hungry. He then described heaven as looking exactly the same. Heaven had the same banquet room with the same feasts and table settings, except, the people at this table were happy, well fed and laughing. What was the difference? The people at the table in hell had four-foot knives and forks strapped to their wrists and were unable to manipulate them to feed themselves. So, they remained gaunt and hungry. The people at the table in heaven also had the four-foot knives and forks strapped to their wrists. But instead of trying to manipulate those knives and forks to feed only themselves, they were feeding each other. Since the table was filled with the abundance of the universe, there was more than enough for everyone. Therefore, everyone was happy and well fed. It is important for you to realize that you are living in a universe governed by laws and regardless of your experience, things happen only as a result of a cause. You cannot receive without first giving and what you receive is in direct proportion to the extent of the giving of your thoughts, time, and abilities.

Proper creative thought, backed up with the appropriate action, opens a doorway for the universe to reciprocate with unlimited abundance. All that is good, fine, and wonderful in your world is yours to have and enjoy. The more you awaken to the divine energies flowing through you and creatively express yourself in a positive manner, the more you will surround yourself with people, places, situations, and things that contribute to the richer experiences of life. Your thoughts and actions are causative factors to which the universe must respond with corresponding effect, such as a stress-less existence.

Affirmation for the day:

I no longer wait for the world to give me what I need. I know that this has already been done for me. I recognize that I am responsible for my experiences and I now commune with Infinite Creator's creative forces and they are acting in and through me. I now consciously acknowledge this. My thoughts and actions express my belief and as I give myself to life, I am abundantly rewarded. I decree it; I believe it, and it is so.

Day Seven:

Just as the universal laws are governing the universe, they are, in some way or another, governing every aspect of your daily living. The universe does not operate in chaos, it operates in

unity, and the laws maintain this unity. In no way

do they, or will they ever, conflict with each other.

You'll soon discover that it doesn't matter what your experiences may be, whether you are concerned with your health, success, affairs or relationships, there is a Universal Law at work. It is you who determines the way the laws work through you and you who determines how you experience them. Things just don't happen without some expression of energy manifesting them! There is always a cause and an effect, an action, and a reaction.

The universal laws can't be avoided or escaped. I have seen far too many times where people think that the laws are working in some cases and not in others. Whether you fully recognize it or not, universal law functions in everything you do. The law is impersonal. It is not concerned with whether you may or may not recognize it; nor is it interested in how you are using it. It has no conscience or concept of what is right and what is wrong; it just is. Therefore, if you are hungry and preparing to cook your last egg and accidentally drop it, the law of gravity does not go "Oops, this is the last egg and this person is hungry, so I won't allow it to drop and break. Instead, I'll place it back in this poor hungry person's hand." The law simply is. If you drop the egg, it will fall, and the odds are very high that it will break.

Did you realize that there is nothing in the universe that decrees that you should be sick or poor or unhappy? Contrary to popular belief, Infinite Creator does not favor one person over another and give one a good life and the other a miserable life. It would be impossible for the Universal Laws that manifests through law and order a good life for one, but not the other. So, if you feel that life is withholding something from you, it is nothing more than the result of your lack of communion with Infinite Creator's ever flowing creative force. All of Infinite Creator's abundance is available to you, but the question is how much of it are you taking? Any law, poorly used, will bring poor results.

In the physical world, scientists are able to give themselves the power of nature only when they are able to understand the laws of nature and their correct use. You are in pretty much the same situation when it comes to the Universal Laws. You have to discover for yourself the nature of the Universal Laws and use them properly. Once you understand that everything is not against you, or out of your hands, and you, and only you, are the one controlling your thinking, actions, and habits, then you can work in cooperation of the Universal Laws and change those patterns. By doing this, you will be able to make your life healthy, happy, prosperous, and stress free!

Affirmation for the day:

I release any and all concepts and ideas that are or have been detrimental to my highest good and I replace them with beneficial ones. Through this action, I work in cooperation with the creative laws and I have a life that is enjoyable. I am happy, healthy, prosperous, and stress free. I decree it; I believe it, and it is so.

Another way to retrain your mode of thinking is through the affirmations of religious quotes. Since the purpose of this book is to guide you along your path of self-discovery and empower you toward a more stress less existence, and not to convert you to any particular religious affiliation, I have taken some quotes from The Holy Bible, the Bhagavad-Gita, and the Urnatia Book. Please take a moment to read the following quotes. At the end of each quote is an affirmation you may be able to associate with. Meditate on the quote and affirmation that feels right to you. It's a marvelous exercise.

The King James Version of the Holy Bible *(Ref. Source: Wikipedia)* ***The Bible*** *is a collection of sacred texts or scriptures that Jews and Christians consider to be a product of divine inspiration and a record of the relationship between God and humans. Many different authors contributed to the Bible. What is regarded as canonical text differs depending on traditions and groups; a number of Bible canons have evolved, with overlapping and diverging contents. The Christian Old Testament overlaps with the Hebrew Bible and the Greek Septuagint; the Hebrew Bible is known in Judaism as the Tanakh. The New Testament is a collection of writings by early Christians, believed to be mostly Jewish disciples of Christ, written in first-century Koine Greek. These early Christian Greek writings consist of narratives, letters, and apocalyptic writings. Among Christian denominations* *there is some disagreement about the contents of the canon, primarily the Apocrypha, a list of works that are regarded with varying levels of respect.*

Day One:

Malachi 3:10... prove me now herewith, saith the Lord of hosts, if I will not open you the windows of heaven and pour you out a blessing, that there shall not be enough room to receive it.

Affirmation:

I affirm that with every thought that I think, I give testimony to my beliefs. I think only positive thoughts, allowing only the good into my existence. I decree it; I believe it, and it is so.

Day two:

Galatians 5:22-23 ... The fruit of the Spirit is
love, joy, peace...gentleness,
goodness, faith... against such there is no law.

Affirmation:

I affirm that Infinite Creator provides my every need. He radiates love, peace, and happincss. I open my life to receive his gifts, allowing them to flow into my life in abundance. I decree it; I believe it, and it is so.

Day three:

Proverbs 3:13 ... Happy is the man that findeth wisdom, and the man that gettteth understanding.

Affirmation:

I affirm that I joyfully accept each experience in my life as a lesson for my personal growth. I decree it; I believe it, and it is so.

Day four:

Colossians 3:10 ... Put on the new man, which is renewed in knowledge after the image of him that created him.

Affirmation:

I affirm that even as the universe is right and perfect, I accept only right and perfect in my reality. I no longer acknowledge, accept, or allow dis-ease of any kind in my existence. I decree it; I believe it,

and it is so.

Day five:

11 Samuel 22:33 ... God is my strength and power: and he maketh my way perfect.

Affirmation:

I affirm that through my divine connection with my Creator, I experience only right and perfect for my daily path. I decree it; I believe it, and it is so.

Day six:

John 5:4... Whatsoever is born of God overcometh the world: and this is the victory that overcometh the world, even our faith.

Affirmation:

I affirm that I am a child of Infinite Creator,

through him I find harmony and balance in my daily living. I decree it; I believe it, and it is so.

Day seven:

Matthew 4:48... Be ye therefore perfect, even as your Father which is in heaven is perfect.

Affirmation:

I affirm that I accept in my life only that which is perfect, as was the intent of my creator. I recognize that dis-ease is allowed by me, and not by Infinite Creator. I cast out all dis-ease and manifest only perfect wholeness in my life and in my body. I decree it; I believe it, and it is so.

The Bhagavad-Gita *(Ref. Source: Wikipedia) The* ***Bhagavad Gita*** *is a 700 verse Hindu scripture in Sanskrit that is part of the Hindu epic Mahabharata (chapters 23–40 of the 6th book of Mahabharata). The Gita is set in a narrative framework of a dialogue between Pandava prince Arjuna and his guide and charioteer Lord Krishna. Facing the duty as a warrior to fight the Dharma Yudhha or righteous war between Pandavas and Kauravas, Arjuna is counselled by Lord Krishna to "fulfill his Kshatriya (warrior) duty as a warrior and establish Dharma." Inserted in this appeal to kshatriya dharma (chivalry) is "a dialogue ... between diverging attitudes concerning methods toward the attainment of liberation (moksha)" The Bhagavad Gita presents a synthesis of the concept of Dharma, theistic bhakti, the yogic ideals of moksha through jnana, bhakti, karma, and Raja Yoga (spoken of in the 6th chapter) and Samkhya philosophy. It is a Bhagavata explanation of the Purusha Sukta and the Purushamedha Srauta yajna described in the Satapatha Brahmana.*

Day one:

Ch.3:28... One who is in knowledge of the Absolute Truth, O mighty-armed, does not engage himself in the senses and sense gratification, knowing well the difference between work in devotion and work for fruitive results.

Affirmation:

I affirm that I know and understand fully my relationship to Infinite Creator. I allow Infinite Creator's creative energies to flow freely through my being, knowing that the right and perfect shall result, as I follow my inner guidance in right actions. I decree it; I believe it, and it is so.

Day two:

Ch2:15... O best among men..., the person who is not disturbed by happiness and distress and

is steady in both, is certainly eligible for liberation.

Affirmation:

I affirm that I remain balanced, knowing that when life is in balance there is no dis-ease. I accept and allow the energies of the universe to flow through me with ease and grace, creating a life of freedom from dis-ease. I decree it; I believe it, and it is so.

Day three:

Ch3:42: ... The working senses are superior to dull matter; mind is higher than the senses; intelligence is still higher than the mind; and he [the soul] is even higher than the intelligence.

Affirmation:

I affirm that as I connect with my innermost highest self, I connect to the avenue leading to Infinite Creator. I seek this connection diligently, knowing that in this, I am whole. I decree it; I believe it, and it is so.

Day four:

Ch4: Being freed from attachment, fear, and anger, being fully absorbed in me, and taking refuge in me, many, many persons in the past became purified, and thus they all attain transcendental love for me.

Affirmation:

I affirm that I remain a clear channel of Infinite Creator's universal energy. By doing this, I eliminate all fear and anger, knowing that these emotions are negative and do not serve me. I pull to me the positive flow of the divine and remain connected, therefore enlightened, and empowered. I decree it; I believe it, and it is so

Day five:

Ch18:45 By following his qualities of work, every man can become perfect...

Affirmation:

I affirm that I connect with Infinite Creator in all that I do. Knowing that by doing this, all results are right and perfect for my life experience. I believe

it. I decree it; I believe it, and it is so

Day six:

Ch13:13...I shall now explain to you the knowable; knowing which you will taste the eternal. This is beginning less and subordinate to me. It is called Brahman, the spirit, and it lies beyond the cause and effect of this material world.

Affirmation:

I affirm that by connecting with my inner self, I am connecting with the all-knowing truth. In this truth, I find life. In this life, I find peace, happiness, health, and prosperity. I decree it; I believe it, and it is so.

Day seven:

Ch7: According to one's existence under the various modes of nature, one evolves a particular kind of faith. The living being is said to be of a particular faith according to the modes that he has acquired.

AFFIRMATION:

I affirm that I am free from confusions of thought and tradition and I allow growth into my very existence. I accept knowledge as my divine right and allow my interpretation and beliefs to flow with the growth of my knowledge. I decree it; I believe it, and it is so.

The Urantia Book: *(Ref. Source: Wikipedia)* ***The Urantia Book*** *is a spiritual and philosophical book that originated in Chicago sometime between 1924 and 1955. The authorship remains a matter of speculation. The authors introduce the word "Urantia" as the name of the planet Earth and state that their intent is to "present enlarged concepts and advanced truth. The book aims to unite religion, science and philosophy, and its enormous amount of material about science is unique among literature claimed to be presented by celestial beings. Among other* *topics, the book discusses the origin and meaning of life, humankind's place in the universe, the relationship between God and people, and the life of Jesus.*

Day one:

PG 8: 1: ... Body, The material or physical

organism of man. The living electrochemical mechanism of animal nature and origin.

Affirmation:

I affirm that as my body is a manifestation of matter in the material form, so are my surroundings. I recognize my inherent abilities of manifestation and I use them to create only positive surroundings. I decree it; I believe it, and it is so.

Day two:

Pg8:2 Mind. The thinking, perceiving, and feeling mechanism of the human organism. The total conscious and unconscious experience. The intelligence associated with the emotional life reaching upward through worship and wisdom to the spirit level.

Affirmation:

I affirm that through connection of Mind, I work with spirit, bringing forth only what is right and perfect. I decree it; I believe it, and it is so.

DAY THREE:

Pg8:3 The divine spirit that indwell the mind of man - the Thought adjuster. This immortal spirit is prepersonal - not personality, though destined to become a part of the personality of the surviving mortal creature.

Affirmation:

I affirm that I recognize my spirit as being immortally connected to the divine. I pull to me the universal knowledge that is mine by divine right, aiding me on my journey toward the highest vibration, while housed within my physical body. I decree it; I believe it, and it is so.

Day four:

Pg. 1119: par 4... Infinite Creator is so all-real and absolute that no material sign of proof or no demonstration of so-called miracle may be offered in testimony of his reality. Always will we know him because we trust him, and our belief in him is wholly based on your personal participation in the divine manifestations of his infinite reality.

Affirmation:

I affirm through faith trust and positive thinking, I'm in receipt of divine blessings. I decree it; I believe it, and it is so.

Day five:

Pg. 1153: par 4...When you stand in awe of the magnitude of the master universe, pause to consider that, even this inconceivable creation can be no more than a partial revelation of the infinite.

Affirmation:

I affirm that Infinite Creator's universal abundance is infinite. It flows around me, through me and to me. It is mine. I release any man-made restrictions that may hinder a clear path for it to flow. I decree it; I believe it, and it is so.

Day six:

Pg. 1445: par3: The Lord is near all who call upon him in sincerity and truth...No good thing will Infinite Creator withhold from those who walk uprightly...

Affirmation:

I affirm that I stand and bathe in the light of Infinite Creator's love, knowing that through him all my needs are met.

I decree it; I believe it, and it is so.

Day seven:

Pg1446: par 5: By your efforts to make amends for past sins you acquire strength to resist future tendencies thereto.

Affirmation:

I affirm that I learn from each mistake that occurs in my life. I see the truth in my actions and I repeat only that which is right and perfect for my highest good. I decree it; I believe it, and it is so

When you are learning to manifest a stress-less lifestyle, it is important to build up your confidence level and your faith in your connection to Infinite Creator's creative energies. I suggest that you make a list of all of the things you would like to manifest. Now is a time to be extensive and not hold back. Remember that you are entitled to abundance in all areas of your life, so don't analyze whether you deserve them or not. Just write down what you feel you would like to accomplish or manifest in your life. Next, arrange them in the order according to their importance in your life, as it stands right now. (Note, as your life changes, so will the order of importance with the list of manifestation "to do's") Now, look at the list and decide which thing you feel would be the easiest to manifest. Don't worry as to whether it is the most important, just as to whether it is the easiest. Now, work on manifesting it. When you have obtained it, cross it off and look again for the easiest thing on the list. Again, cross it off after you have received or achieved it. It may be something very insignificant in the scheme of things, but it is something that you desire and that is the important factor to look at now. When you have accomplished several of the easiest things, go towards the more important things on your list and pick the one that seems to be the easiest from that section. Again, cross it off when you have obtained success in manifesting it and continue. The more things you are able to cross off the list, the more confidence you will have that you can complete it and the more balanced and stress-free your life will become.

When manifesting, it is sometimes good to have a blueprint of how you will manifest it. Start making plans for how you will accomplish the one on the top of your list and write it down. Look at it daily while you continue to work on the rest of the list. When you feel confident and ready, tackle Number One! Don't be discouraged about the time frame of working your way through the list. Be realistic and patient with yourself and most of all stay calm and relaxed. If the task of manifestation feels stressful to you, then perhaps you are not really supposed to manifest that particular thing or situation at that particular time, if ever. Stop and move on to the next one on your list and go back later to see if it is easier to manifest later.

CLEANSING

WE HAVE ALREADY ACKNOWLEDGED the fact that you, and everything on earth, including the earth, are made of energy; and energy vibrates. The famous MD, Deepak Chopra, writes and lectures on the theory of this point when he focuses on quantum physics. Without getting into the theory of quantum physics (if you would like to read Dr. Chopra's works on this, an excellent book is "Ageless Body, Timeless Mind") I will focus on the fact that all matter absorbs vibration. Because of this, the energy field will be filled with the most dominant vibration. This is why you will experience good and peaceful sensations when you enter a church or are in the presence of a member of the cloth. Both the church and the clergy are constantly being reinforced with the positive energy vibration of the universe through thought, prayer

and material means.

When you are cleansing a home, your body, or even your mind's thoughts, what you are doing, in essence, is shifting the dominant vibrations. This will give whatever is being cleansed a more desirable "feel" for you. Cleansing brings balance back, thus lessening the effects of daily stress and allowing you to manifest good into your life.

When you are preparing to manifest, you should first do a cleansing to open the avenue for the desired manifestation to flow through to your reality.

We are taught in the Christian Holy Scriptures two very powerful manifestation prayers; although they may not have been perceived as such throughout the ages. But let's look at them. You will find my input or suggestion for interpretation in italics under each line.

THE LORD'S PRAYER

1] Our Father

The ONE who created us

2] Which art in heaven

Heaven being eternity and the space beyond our reality as we see it presently

3] Hollowed be Thy name

We revere the sanctity of Infinite Creator

4] Thy kingdom come

We are striving for the perfection of the Christ and to be able to dwell in the presence of Infinite Creator.

5] Thy will be done, on earth, as it is in heaven

The workings of the divine are not reserved for the heavenly spheres, as the kingdom of the holy is here on earth and the will or power or desire or ability is here as well.

6] Give us this day our daily bread and forgive us our debts as we forgive our debtors.

Help us today to live and grow (for bread represents the manna of life) and help us to release any karma we may have with others or them with us... thus enhancing the process of receiving Infinite

Creator's divine energy.

7] And lead us no into temptation but deliver us from evil.

Help us to remember what we forgot when we re-incarnated, that we may tap into the universal well of knowledge. (Evil equals ignorance)

8] For Thine is the kingdom and the power, and the glory forever. AMEN

For all things are of Infinite Creator. So Be It.

THE TWENTY THIRD PSALM

1] The Lord is my shepherd

Infinite Creator is watching over me and guiding me, (much as in biblical times the shepherd was caring for his flocks of sheep).

2] I shall not want.

The abundance of the universe is available to me; therefore, I lack for nothing.

3] He maketh me to lie down in green pastures.

I am provided with the opportunity for fertile

growth and abundance.

4] He leadeth me besides the still waters

When communing with Infinite Creator, I find peace and tranquility.

5] He restoreth my soul.

My soul is in the care of Infinite Creator, ever rejuvenated

6] He leadeth me in the paths of righteousness for his name's sake.

The guidance to the Christ light is ever available.

7] Yea, though I walk through the valley of the shadow of death, I will fear no evil.

Death is not to be feared, for it is a positive transformation.

8] For Thou art with me,

And Infinite Creator's presence is never ending

9] Thy rod and Thy staff they comfort me.

I have the ability to use the tools and gifts of heaven to assist me at will.

10] Thou preparest a table before me in the presence of mine enemies.

The opportunity for protection and care is ever present, always available, should I choose to partake.

11] Thou anointest my head with oil.

I am Divinely blessed.

12] My cup runneth over

There is more available to me than I could every use, complete abundance is mine.

13] Surely goodness and mercy shall follow me all the days of my life and I shall dwell in the house of the Lord forever. Amen

Throughout my life I will have available to me the blessings and gifts of the universe, they are at my disposal for eternity. So Be It.

The following are more modern prayers. They

use the form of affirmations and assurance that we are all in possession of the rights and privileges as cocreators of our reality.

One

I command White Fire and Violet flames to surround me! Cleansing, purifying, uplifting, balancing, healing, and protecting me now! I command an armor of silver and violet flames in the shape of an egg! In this armor I am invincible, and impenetrable! Only Infinite Creator and good may enter my armor of Light. So be it, as I have decreed it.

Two

[Say the following three times, while visualizing a circle of light enfolding you]

Circle of light. Barrier of all that is evil... Activate now!

Three

The light of Infinite Creator surrounds me,

The love of Infinite Creator enfolds me,

The presence of Infinite Creator watches over me,

The power of Infinite Creator protects me, Wherever I am, Infinite Creator is.

Any of these can be used in preparation for a cleansing or meditation or further prayer or as a daily shield against negativity before resuming your activities.

Cleansing your outside body

I am sure you'll be able to think back and remember a point and time when you were in the presence of another individual and felt the energy, even after that person left. Or you have entered a room or an area that may have felt wonderful, eerie, or just unclean, and you still experienced that sensation after leaving.

What happened is that the energy of that person or area or room has mixed and mingled with your own energy field and has left a residue. This is all well and good if the energy is delightfully positive. But if it is not, after a while the buildup can prove to be overwhelming. This is the reason many people become imbalanced, irritable, tired, and eventually ill. It all starts in the energy field of the body, better known as the aura. It is very important to keep your auric field clean and balanced. It is in this field that dis-ease first takes hold. If left long enough, dis-ease can become disease. The following are some suggestions for cleaning your auric field:

1. Daily shower. (How simple is that?) This will remove most of the incompatible energy, but you will find that if the imbalance has already been created, [a result of a long time between the experience and the opportunity to shower], it may not be enough.

2. Bathe in sea salt. If there is no sea salt available, Epsom salt will act as a suitable substitute. This will alter the electrodes in your energy field and neutralize any negativity. It brings your polarities back into balance.

3. Bathe in Goats milk. Not only is this believed to be excellent for removing negativity and balancing the polarities, but also it is great for the skin! (Just a tablespoon or two of powdered goat's milk in your bath water does it!)

4. Smudge yourself. The use of the sage herb, when dried and smoking will balance and cleanse your energy field nicely. You may also use cedar if you find sage offensive. Most westerners will use Native American sage, but I prefer

Eastern Indian sage, which can be found in Indian food stores in large bags for a very economical cost.

Cleansing your inside body

Although this is a longer process of at least thirty to sixty days, depending upon the severity of your situation, it is a very necessary part of body maintenance. If you are clean on the outside, but filled with toxins inside, your energy will be out of balance, making it far more difficult to manifest your desires. My favorite blood cleaner is Chlorella. It works slowly, but since it runs through the systemic organs, you'll eventually find balance. Bentonite clay combined with Senna or Psyllium Husks will do an excellent job with colon cleansing; but can be harsh and should be done on a limited basis, if at all. There are many pre-mixed formulas in most reputable health food stores that will save you the mess and guess of mixing on your own. (Follow instructions to the letter!) You'll also find a variety of foods and supplements later in this book that will help with inner body maintenance. For those of you who don't want to ingest a colon cleanse, a colonic works wonders.

Cleansing a room

There is more than one reason to cleanse a room. The primary reason would be that the materials in the room (walls, floor, furniture) are porous and will absorb the energy and, depending upon what has been occurring in the room, you may have vibrations not to your liking. If there has been heavy arguing, an act of violence, theft, illness, a lot of stress experienced, etc., the room will hold the vibrations. Positive promotes positive. Negative promotes negative. Negative also provides a compatible environment for entities that are of a lesser vibration to harbor. This is another reason for cleansing a home or a building.

An excellent way to tell if the vibrations of a building are in order is to observe the plant life in it. If the plants are thriving, then all is well. If not, then it is a fairly good indication that it is time to do a cleansing.

To cleanse a room, you can do one or more of the following:

1] Repeatedly pray in the room

2] Smudge the room

3] Spray the room with sea salt and water while burning purified white candles.

4] Wash the room with ammonia and water, then sprinkle sea salt in its corners.

Note: I recommend that you limit your cleansing to room balancing only in the beginning. If you feel you have an unwanted entity in the room, it is advisable to call in someone who has a greater knowledge and understanding.

ANGELS AND SPIRITS

I'M SURE THAT YOU ARE curious about why I have included the next few topics in a book that is supposed to be about stress management. The answer is very simple. I'm focusing on stress of all levels; body, mind, and spirit. The pragmatic, day to day stress of living, coping with and manifesting is the most apparent stress, of course. But there are millions of people, like myself, having daily encounters with the spirit realm, angelic realm, and metaphysical realm, who are just as confused and stressed out by it; as I was for so many years. By bringing clarity and understanding in this area, you will be able to alleviate or eliminate a great deal of emotional stress from your life. I'll begin with angels.

Angels have been with us throughout time. Our ancestors, through the ages, have tried to pass

on what they knew to be true through stories and folklore. We find record of them in biblical scripture, in paintings and poetry.

Since the discovery of science, these stories and records have become considered more lore than fact. If you can't see it through a microscope or a telescope, then it must not exist, right? Wrong. This new, scientific thought trend does not erase the existence of the angelic realm. Believers in angels recognize that just because it cannot be seen, does not mean that it does not exist. A good example of a person not experiencing something that is very real, is the dog whistle. When you blow it, you hear nothing, yet the dog responds. Does this mean that the whistle sound doesn't exist? Or how about the age-old question, "When a tree falls in the middle of a forest and there is no one there to witness it, does it still make a sound?" My point is that the existence of something is not dependent upon whether you are astute enough to be aware of it.

You'll find in all of the scriptures of the major religions of the Western world, Christianity, Judaism, and Islam, as well as other religious sects, repeated references of angelic interventions. All of these writings seem to agree that there are many different types of heavenly beings bridging the spiritual and physical realms. The opinions as to how many exist and what they are named, or what functions they perform, are varied. I, of course, can only share with you what I have learned.

Generically "angel" refers to all heavenly beings. Specifically, it is a term referring to the members of the third sphere, or the sphere closest to the physical realm. The term "archangel" again is often used generically to refer to all of the higher orders of heavenly beings, but the archangels are actually one of the orders.

The following is the order of angelic beings, in accordance to my learning:

Angels that serve as heavenly counselors; commonly called 1st. sphere:

1] Seraphim

2] Cherubim

3] Thrones

Angels that work as heavenly governors; commonly called 2nd sphere:

1] Dominions

2] Virtues

3] Powers

Angels that function as heavenly messengers; commonly called the 3rd sphere:

1] Principalities

2] Archangels

3] Angels

The angels that we are most commonly aware of are the last order, simply; angels. They are the beings who are the closest to humans and are the most concerned with our affairs. Within this category, are many different kinds of angels; each with its own function.

Just beyond the angels are the archangels. They are involved with the larger scope of things and are commonly referred to as the over-lighting angels. The archangels are a different family from the angels and, again, there are many different kinds. The most familiar archangels are Gabriel, Michael,

Rafael, and Uriel.

Principalities are the next sphere or level of

angels. They are the guardian angels of all the large groups on earth, such as cities and nations and other human creations like multinational corporations.

These angels could accurately be referred to as Integrating angels. There are many of these angels involved with planet earth.

The first order in this level or sphere is known as the Powers. They are the bearers of the conscience of all of humanity. The Powers are the keepers of collective history. Within this category you will find the angels of death and the angels of birth. They are able to draw down and hold the energy of the Divine plan the same way that trees draw down the energy of the sun. In this way, the Powers can send everyone visions of world spirituality networking.

The next group beyond the Powers is the group of the Virtues. They are of particular importance today because they are able to project massive levels of Divine energy. There will be a greater infusion of spiritual energy for our planet and the negative net that has formed will be transmuted to positive energy as more groups of people learn to work with the Virtues.

The Dominions are the heavenly beings who

govern the activities of the other angelic groups lower in the realms. They are the divine bureaucrats and also work to integrate the spiritual and material worlds. Dominions receive their orders from Infinite Creator, and rarely have contact with individuals. Even so, their work is still connected to your reality.

The third sphere is the Thrones. They are the companion angels of the planets. The Earth Angel is the most influential one for us and is the guardian angel of our planet.

Next are the Cherubim, the guardians of light and the stars. Although remote from our plane of reality, their light still touches our lives. It is the Divine light of heaven.

Finally, the highest order is the order of the Seraphim who are said to surround the throne of our Creator. They sing the music of the spheres and regulate the movement of the heavens as it emanates from Infinite Creator.

The angels have cousins called the Nature Spirits.

The nature spirits are themselves an angelic

order but are on a different wavelength from their angelic cousins. Some of the names most commonly used to refer to the Nature Spirits from different cultures are: Devas, Elves, Fairies, Undines, Sylphs, Salamanders, Fauns, Trolls, and Gnomes. These spirits are the presiding beings that oversee all living and growing things, such as crops, gardens, forests and lakes, animals, fish, and fowl.

You can find their work in flocks of birds, schools of fish, down to the simple delicacy of a single leaf.

Nature spirits co-create and nurture the physical environment and don't require the assistance of man. People who have sensitive abilities and work with the land have acknowledged their existence and seen the value in working with them. Whether you are aware of it or not, you connect with the nature spirits whenever you tend to your plants, walk in the woods or a garden, hug a tree or eat anything that has been grown.

Our human bodies also have Nature Spirits,

or Devas (pronounced day-vahs), as they are most commonly referred to. The Devas of your body coordinates the incredible amount of information constantly flowing through you. They are the spiritual equivalent of the myriad of cells, microorganism and organisms that cooperate in such conglomerates as your kidneys, lever, lungs, heart, and pancreas, to mention a few.

Of all of the angelic beings, the nature spirits are the ones who are most closely tuned into your human reality. They should be respected, since they carry the burden of most of your environmental mishaps; yet they are more than willing to serve. Opening yourself to them now is very important since they possess information needed at this time for our planet's transformation.

It is common for man to project his human traits and characteristics upon the angels. Man sees and understands things in a very different perspective than angels do. Even so, they have man's higher goals in common.

You can find a large amount of contradictory information in angelic lore. I'm sharing with you what I have learned and believe to be true, but it may conflict with what you may hear, read, or learn in from others. This is normal, since again, we all perceive differently. I suggest you take, from what you read, what feels right and perfect for your

Reality and go from there.

Some believe that the angel is immortal, while

others claim that they are created only for a specific time and a specific function. People disagree over when they were created, whether or not they have free will (I was taught they do not, by the way), if they have physical bodies and whether people can become angels after they die. (It is my understanding the we are spirits which are a different breed than angels and very rarely do we change breed) Some question whether angels are an aspect of our soul. I feel that there is no correct way to experience angels and there is no right or wrong way to see them either. Angels will manifest in a manner that is easiest for you, as an individual, to perceive.

The next time you take the time to meditate, why not connect with your own personal guardian angel and begin a journal? You will be both delighted and surprised by the myriad of ways the angels will appear to you and the many messages you will receive to assist you with your highest good.

The stressful task of daily living can be overwhelming, especially when you feel you are alone. It is important to remember that you are anything but alone! You have angels around you always and you should feel free to call upon these angels for assistance with your daily activities and duties.

Although it is nice and often comforting to know the names and primary functions of the angels, it is not necessary to call them by name, since they respond to the vibration of desire. 'Ask and ye shall receive.' When you desire with a purity of heart, you are asking! But, although you don't need to know their names, I feel that understanding the different categories of angels will help you to focus more clearly.

Here are some helpful categories of angels.

Angel of Grace: The Angels of Grace work is constant as they weave together the spiritual and material realms. When you cross their path, you are woven into their work and for an instant experience the intensity of universal love and you are gifted with grace. As an example: You may glimpse moments of joy when experiencing sorrow. Such is the working of an Angel of Grace. The more aware you are of their presence, the more sensitive

and open you become to them at all times.

Angel of Peace: Peace is the harmony of energy that permeates the universe. The Angels of Peace carry the vision and the energy for the transformation of an Angel of Grace.

Attunement Angel: Attunement angels are also called Ceremonial or Ritual Angels and are concerned with time. Although they are available to you anytime, they come to you when you are praying or meditating and attune you to the sacredness of the moment.

Companion Angel: This angel works with you on an intimate level in all life situations, as your personal angel and beloved friend. Another term for Companion Angel is Guardian Angel. If you open yourself up to your companion angel's presence, you will find yourself filled with a sense of peace, love and joy and wisdom.

Connecting Angel: The Connecting Angel, sometimes referred to as the Collective Angel is the guardian angel for groups and relationships. Whenever people gather together, one of these angels is drawn to work with them and to help them to connect their energies and their intentions. Depending upon the time frame of the relationship, a Connecting Angel may stay around for a long or short period of time.

Dream Angel: The Dream Angel is related to the Information Angel. The difference is that this angel works with you when you are sleeping, rather than when you are awake. Since their specialty is the unconscious state, the Dream Angel is the attendant in altered states of consciousness such as trances and out of body experiences

Healing Angel: The Healing Angel awakens the healer in you. They are with you to assist in facilitating healing on all levels. You will find them in hospitals and around medical and healing practitioners.

Information Angel: The Information Angel is also known as the Wisdom Angel. The function of this angel is to provide information to anyone who asks for it. They are the universal librarians and the keepers of the Akashic records. (A spiritual recording of all that ever was and all that will be.) The Information Angel may present information to you directly or simply fill you with inspiration. It is common for these angels to work with you directly, guiding you to toward the information you seek. An example of how they work is, a song that will not leave your head, a book that falls off a shelf, or a movie that you stumble on while surfing television channels in the middle of a sleepless night.

Nature Angel: These angels work with the four elements of nature; earth, water, fire, and air. The Nature Spirits are included in this category. These angels are concerned with forms of life from the most minute to the grand, from flowers to trees.

Transformational Angel: Also called the Manifestation Angels, the Transformational Angel is responsible for the transformation of spirit and thought into the physical realm. Prosperity Angels are part of this category of angels. The Transformational Angel assists you whenever you are doing creative work. They work with the higher angels of birth and death as well.

Here is a list of the most known angels and a description of their function that I have compiled from my studies. Although they are the most known, they are by no means more important than the others. They all serve in an important way. Getting familiar with them and the concept of working with them aids in reducing stress and that sense of being alone.

Ariel, whose meaning is "Lion of God," is ranked as one of the seven princes who ruled the waters. He is also known as the Earth's Great Lord. In Gnostic the beliefs, Ariel is the angel who controls the demons. Ariel has also been associated with the order of angels referred to as the Thrones. He was known to have assisted the archangel Rafael in the curing of diseases.

Gabriel, whose name means "God is my strength," appears out of the higher realm to be the most frequently recorded visitor. In biblical times, Mary and Elizabeth were surprised with his announcements of the births of their sons Jesus and John the Baptist. In Islam, Gabriel is the considered the Spirit of Truth who dictated the Quran to their Profit Mohammed. And in Jewish belief, Gabriel parted the waters of the Red Sea so that the Hebrews could escape the Pharaoh's soldiers. It was Gabriel who also appeared to Joan of Arc and inspired her to go to the aid of the dauphin. Gabriel is the planet's heavenly angel of vibratory transformation.

Melchizedek, who is also known as the Sage of Salem is another of the less well-known angels who has taken human, very male form. According to the Urantia book, he appeared in full form about 2,000 years before the arrival of Jesus and announced that he was a servant of El Elyon, the Most High. Melchizedek set up a teaching center of which he personally oversaw for approximately ninety years. It was Melchizedek who delivered Infinite Creator's covenant to Abraham and introduced the concept of Salvation through pure faith of the thinking of the planet earth. Melchizedek formed a wide missionary program, centered in Salem (the ancient site of Jerusalem) which sent out thousands of missionaries who literally circled the globe. In Phoenician mythology, Melchizedek was believed to be the father of the seven Elohim. In the third century AD a group of "heretics" who called themselves the Melchisidans, claimed to be in touch with a great power named Melchizedek and this power was greater than Christ was. His service here as the Sage of Salem was said to have been an effort of the behalf of the celestials to bring some much-needed light to a dark and chaotic time and to set the seeds for the coming of the great Christ.

Metatron is considered one of the greatest of all the angels. He is honored as the chief of the ministering angels, the chief recording angel, chancellor of heaven and the angel by whom the world is maintained. And so mighty that he possesses seventy-two other names. He was supposedly once a humble mortal being, the patriarch Enoch. According to lore, Enoch earned such merit in the eyes of the Lord for his goodness and abilities as a scribe that he was taken to heaven, an event noted in the Book of Genesis (5:24). One of Metatron's most dramatic achievements involved two evil Egyptian sorcerers who used their advanced knowledge of magic to ascend to heaven. Such was their strength that neither Michael nor Gabriel could expel them. Metatron, however, broke their spells and cast out the impudent Egyptians. For this reason, Metatron is considered by some to be superior to most of the angels, including Michael, Gabriel, and Uriel.

Michael, whose name means "Who is like God" is the best known of the archangels. Michael is acknowledged by all three of the most prominent western religions. He is believed to have appeared to Moses as the fire in the burning bush and to have rescued Daniel and his friends from the lion's den. To the Christians, he is the angel who informed Mary of her approaching death. In Islam, we are told that his wings are the color of "green emerald and are covered with saffron hairs, each of them containing a million faces, mouths and tongues which, in a million dialects, implore the pardon of Allah." The Quran also depicts an image of the Cherubim being formed from the tears of Michael. In the Dead Sea Scrolls, Michael emerges, fighting a war against the Sons of Darkness as the Prince of Light, where he leads the angelic battle against the legions of the fallen angel Belial. Michael was declared to be the patron of all policemen by Pope Pius XII.

Moroni is the angel primarily recognized by the Church of Jesus Christ of Latter Day Saints. In 1823, it's reported that the Angel Moroni appeared to the prophet Joseph Smith in Palmyra, New York. He guided Joseph in his discovery of buried golden tablets that were inscribed with dense lettering. Moroni helped Joseph Smith translate these tablets. This translation is now known as the Book of Mormon. This book tells us that prior to the destruction of Jerusalem, about 600BC, a Jewish family fled the city and made its way by ship to what is now North America. Their descendants became two nations, of which there was a conflict between and one nation was lost and the other became the ancestor of the Native Americans. Records that were kept by one of the last elders of the vanished nation tell that Jesus appeared to them after his death on the cross. The elder's name was Mormon and it was his son Moroni who buried the tablets his father had kept in about 44 AD. According to the story, Moroni joined the ranks of Enoch and Elijah and was transformed into an angel and follows in the tradition of Gabriel in being the angelic giver of a book of revelations. There is a forty-foot-high statue of Moroni that stands on top of a hill near Palmyra, New York. The angel is shown as he appeared to the prophet, clothed in a long robe with no wings. Moroni was described as" being of light with a face like lightning."

Rafael, whose name means "God has Healed," is depicted in western art as the most endearing of the angels. His image is featured in creations like Botticelli, Titian, and Rembrandt. Rafael is the archangel who is in charge of the healing of earth. There have been stories through the ages of the healing work that was performed by Rafael. It has been reported that when Samuel hurt Jacob's thigh, he was sent by Infinite Creator to cure it. Rafael also healed Abraham's pain from his circumcision and is also reported to have given the "medical book" to Noah after the great flood.

Raziel, meaning "Secret of God," is believed to be an "angel of the secret regions and chief of the supreme mysteries." As legend has it, Raziel is the author of a book "wherein all celestial and earthly knowledge is set down." When Raziel gave his book to Adam, it was stolen by some envious angels and thrown into the ocean, where Rahab, the primordial angel, recovered it and passed it first to Enoch and then to Noah. This book is where Noah got his information on how to build the ark. It's also rumored that Solomon possessed the book. The Zohar, which is associated most often with Jewish mysticism, claims that in the middle of Raziel's book there are secret writings "explaining the fifteen hundred keys to the mystery of the world which were never revealed to the angels," Another belief amongst the Jewish mystics is that each day the angel Raziel proclaims the secrets of men to all

mankind, while standing on Mt. Horeb.

Uriel, whose name means "Fire of God," has confusion around his rank. He is deemed as a seraph, a cherub, a regent of the sun, and the flame of

Infinite Creator who presides over Hades. Uriel's best known as the Archangel of Salvation and is said to be one of the angels of the Presence, which is a very high position, since only the highest voltage angels can sustain the presence of Infinite Creator. Uriel is thought to have been the spirit who "stood at the gate of the lost Eden with the fiery sword."

In the Book of Enoch, Uriel was sent by God to warn Noah of the impending floods. It's also written that Uriel disclosed the mysteries of the heavenly Arcana to Ezra and led Abraham out of Ur in the Chaldeans region. It's been stated that Uriel brought the art of divine alchemy to the planet earth and gave the Hebrews their mystic tradition, the Kabbalah. Uriel has been described as the "sharpest sighted spirit of all in Heaven" and when Moses neglected to circumcise his son Gresham, it was Uriel who chastised him.

Having touched on the topic of Angels, I now move to spirits. I saw a bumper sticker a while back that read *"We are not humans having a spiritual experience; we are spirits having a human experience."* In short, spirits are people without the bodies. Just like humans, spirits have emotions, desires and beliefs and they too have the right to exercise free will. There is a common misconception that when a person dies, or, as I prefer crosses over; the person is immediately an angelic being who is privy to all the secrets of the universe. It is my understanding that, although a person who has made his or her crossing is more aware of the universal truth than when they were in body, he or she does not necessarily have all of the answers to all of the questions.

Death is the separation of your life force from your body, that is all it is. It is an ending of that relationship only. I equate it to graduation from a school of some type. When your education is complete, you leave the school, but you continue on your journey of life. When your body dies, your spirit continues on its journey back to Infinite Creator. You are still able to exercise the options of conscious awareness of right and wrong when you are in spirit form. Spirits can still agree or disagree with what is perceived as reality. Because of this fact, spirits can accept or reject the option of moving forward to the next level of growth in the spiritual realm. Those who have rejected (primarily out of fear) are what is referred to as "earth bound." If you accept, then you raise your vibration awareness and get closer and closer to Infinite Creator's realm and the Christ energy; thus, lessening and eventually eliminating the necessity to obtain and/ or occupy a physical body (reincarnation). If you reject, then you are either caught in the void between the two worlds or thrown down lower in the cycle of reincarnation with limited knowledge. There are some spirits who are so desirous to remain in and attached to the human world that they become angry and resentful when they find themselves removed and "hang around" instead of moving on. Because they keep the basics of their personalities, they are at times unpleasant. These are the spirits that are reported to perform haunting and possession. These are the spirits that are so commonly referred to as ghosts. But, are they really ghosts? A ghost is trapped energy; a spirit is free flowing. This means that a ghost is a spirit who is shocked or died so suddenly that it literally doesn't know what hit it and is therefore not aware that it is dead. A ghost actually becomes entrapped in an energy pocket and continues to act out or play out the part of its reality that it remembers best. This is usually what happened prior to the death of its last human body. These souls generally are grateful to move on as soon as they are made aware of the fact of what has occurred and what the next step should be. Prayer serves as a powerful tool to assist in releasing ghosts from their entrapment.

Occasionally a loved one passes on and his or her spirit remains close to earth as he or she makes attempts to contact the living for one final good-bye or set of instructions. It happens especially if the death was unexpected. These situations would not be considered a haunting. A haunting is done by a spirit that is aware that it has left its body and is either resentful of having to give up the pleasures of the human senses or is afraid. These spirits will also appear in homes and create havoc of all natures as they try to connect with the people and remain in the vibration of earth. Since a haunting is done on a deliberate basis and is done by a spirit, not a ghost, it is much easier to remove a ghost from an environment than it is to remove a spirit who is in haunting mode.

The vibration rate of the spirit's energy will determine whether you are able to see it with your naked eye or not. There have been people who have been able to raise their own body's vibration rate to the point where they are able to see into the spiritual dimension, but usually it is the spirit lowering its vibration rate that allows the visual contact. Keeping this in mind, the next time (or the first time) you see or feel the presence of a spirit, instead of getting stressed out, try talking to it. It may have a conversation waiting for you.

Just like you have guardian angels or companion angels, you also have guardian or companion spirits. As you progress forward with your growth process, so do your companion spirits. They are assigned to you to assist and to aid you with your human experiences while continuing your spiritual path. Consider them like you would a professor at a college, who has already walked the path he is teaching you. He has earned the right to have his Masters, but is still working on his Ph.D. By teaching you what he has learned, he will complete his quest for his own credentials. For this reason, we call your main companion spirit your master teacher.

There are many companion spirits that work with you at one point and level of your life's path, but usually only one master teacher who will be with you from the time you are born until the time you die. This spirit can be your best friend and companion, showing you a delightful zest for life and a sense of humor to the point that you may just forget yourself that it is not housed in a human body. As I stated earlier, Urla - Ra is my personal master teacher, [as well as a teacher to the planet.]

I have often been asked from my students and my clients what culture and race their spirit guide is. Your guide will resonate to you in a manner that you find acceptable. Since they too have gone through the process of reincarnation, they have been many races, colors, and sexes. So, they will appear in a manner that you will accept. I have found that it is generally a life that both of you connect to or resonate with. That is why some people have Egyptian, some Native American and so on.

When you are in meditation, I suggest that you get acquainted with your master teacher. It is a wonderful, comforting, and rejuvenating experience. If you find it difficult at first, I encourage you to keep at it. You are only going to perceive as much as you are capable of at that time. Your guides or your angels will not appear before you, or even communicate openly with you, if they are in the belief that you are not able to cope with it. Any fear will hinder you.

REINCARNATION

[DEATH, REBIRTH & KARMA]

To reiterate on what I stated in the chapter on meditation, science tells you that we are made of energy. Science also tells you that energy cannot be destroyed, it simply takes another form. This is the concept behind reincarnation. There have been, through time, stories about spirits and ghosts, people coming back from the dead and people coming back as new people. As with all lore, they are based on truth. Life is a school where our awareness is every widening. As we develop more and more of our own inherent talents and abilities and get into a deeper and stronger communion with Infinite Creator, the memory banks within our cells open as well. There are two theories as to why we remember past lives. One is the theory that 'thought is energy,' and each thought is stored for eternity in our DNA. As we create new life and give birth to our offspring, these thoughts are passed on with the DNA and therefore, as the person develops, the thoughts are accessible. The other theory is that our spirit continues to be reborn in various bodies, in accordance to the needs of our spiritual growth. I prefer the latter explanation. My reason being is that if an individual is clearly remembering a life as a Native American, or an Eskimo, how do you explain the genetic lineage of South African or Brazilian?

It is my belief and understanding that your spirit comes to the planet earth for learning and progression, such as you would a school. As you progress in spirit, you continue to enter earth-life at a more advanced level, until you reach such a state of knowing and understanding that it allows the option of no longer needing to return. The primary focus is to shorten or eliminate the number of times you must incarnate. This is done by doing the most you possibly can to learn and broaden your understanding in the body that you have right now.

The primary concern that I have encountered from people, when they learn of this philosophy, is "Well, if the person knows they can do it over again, why do they need to worry about being good this lifetime? Why not just enjoy and fornicate ya-de-da... for tomorrow (in this case, next lifetime) I can be good!" (I believe that it was fear and lack of faith in the masses ability to comprehend and do what is right that prompted many religions to remove the concept of reincarnation from their teachings) The reason you would not want to carry on in such a wild and abandoned manner is simple. Karma! Karma is the result of the law of cause and effect. Knowledge of this prevents those who are aware from straying from their path of enlightenment. When you have action, you also have reaction. This makes every move you do and every thought you have very important. For, since thought is energy, if there is enough force behind it, or it is repeated enough, it will be set into motion, an action will occur and will create a reaction. Karma is the law of cause and effect. It is the result of your actions. You can have good karma or negative karma, depending upon your actions. Do you still want to go out there and whoop it up beyond reason and sensibility?

More and more today, as the earth's vibrations speed up, we are seeing and experiencing what is referred to as 'instant karma.' But this does not mean that you are also not dealing with the effects or re-actions (karma) of past lives. You may run into people who have karma with you from another time and are given the opportunity to correct the situation so that you both can move forward.

Understanding what karma is and how do deal with it can ease a tremendous amount of anxiety and stress from a person. Karma is not a negative thing; it just is. What makes it negative is you. If you do something that is going to create harm to another, either emotionally or physically, you will be creating a negative karma for yourself. But just as equally, if you do something that is kind and beneficial for another person, either emotionally or physically, you will be creating positive karma for yourself. The choice is yours. It is important to remember that the law of cause and effect is not just limited to the interaction between people. The law has no conscience and responds to actions only; whether they are actions by man, or beast or thing. Another factor to consider is the power in thought theory. If you "knowingly" create harm or cheat, the force behind the thought will intensify your negative karma. So, think long and hard about something you feel may be harmful to someone (or yourself), before you act! And if you do find that you have slipped up, here is the good news! In some cases, depending upon the karmic debt being paid, you can actually transmute and eliminate negative karma by doing something good that far exceeds the level of vibration of the bad.

Since we are all unique, it stands to reason that we will all experience death in our own way. But, there is a basic pattern or order to things that the majority of spirits who are desirous of progression choose to follow. When you leave your physical body through death, you are offered the opportunity to go into a resting period. This is commonly referred to as the sleep state. The purpose for this resting period is to allow your energy to adjust to not being in a physical body and to again remember expansion. This resting time, in human measurements, is approximately one year. The discriminatory Spiritist will respect that resting period and not connect with or try to channel the individual during that time frame. The Spiritist will also encourage the loved ones who are left behind on earth to release the desire for that person who died to be there with them, hence, lessening the possibility of that spirit being pulled back and hindering its path of progression.

When you awaken from your resting period, or sleep state, you are then reunited with your spiritual companions, teachers, and family. At this time, you will evaluate your progression. You will look back and determine what you learned in your lifetimes. Did you move forward, or did you regress? (That's right. There is always the risk that you will regress instead of progress) By regress, I mean, did you use the laws of the universe in a manner that was beneficial or detrimental to your progression?

The average individual incarnates hundreds of times with a minimum of fifty years in between. This is not written in stone, just what I've been taught to be the average. Once you have had the assistance of a higher spiritual realm in determining what is needed to expand your awareness in spirit, you then select the pattern for your earthly life. You select the genetics, the environment etc. For example, you may place yourself in a situation where you will be genetically fat, abandoned or abused. The purpose of this could be to possibly work through some karma for what you have done or to give yourself an opportunity to learn unconditional love. You sometimes have to learn to give and teach and are placed in a situation where you will do that in the physical body. Some individuals come into life not for themselves, but to offer an opportunity for another to experience and learn; like a young child who dies, offering the parents and other family members and friends the opportunity for growth and understanding through loss. Each lifetime has a learning purpose.

When you enter your body, a veil of forgetfulness is placed over you in accordance to your level of advancement. This veil is necessary because if you did not have it, you would remember what you know to be true and may not be able to experience the lessons intended for you. As you advance and progress in your understanding and vibration toward the Christ energy, you wear a lesser and lesser veil. This explains the many individuals who come to earth advanced and loving. Many of them have been recorded in our history books and religious records.

Up until the age of nine years old, the child's veil is very porous; which keeps them connected to the spiritual world. This explains how children seem to know things and report having "imaginary friends" or that they are seeing people that others cannot see. Thought energy will solidify that veil. So, if the influence on that child promotes enlightenment, it will remain porous, but if the child is conditioned to believe in fear, limitations, and negativity, or is told repeatedly that the spirit world and universal knowledge is taboo, the odds are great that the veil will solidify. The exceptions to this are when the spirit is very advanced and inherently empowered enough to reject the conditioning attempts.

We humans tend to be very sentimental. Because of this, it is very tempting and quite common to fall into the belief pattern that our relatives and friends who have died are now our guardian angels and are devoting their time to watching over us. Although a comforting thought and possibly one that may ease the stress of losing someone from us, it is quite unrealistic. Think about it. Since it is our quest to grow and progress toward the Christ energy state, and in this quest, we have had many physical bodies, wouldn't it make sense that when we leave a body behind and are consciously aware of the need for progression, we focus on that progression? This would therefore require that we either continue our lessons in spirit or reincarnate.

Sometimes part of our spiritual lessons is in fact to communicate with the people we knew in the physical life we recently left; but not always. Our refusal to let go of our loved ones after they have died, and continuing to desire them to be with us, will hinder their progression. You can actually "pull" on their energy with your desire that they return and, if they are truly connected to you, their love will not deny you. Instead, they choose to deny themselves a speedy progression. This is why it is important to release the ones you love and allow them to move forward. This does not mean that you must forget them or stop loving them. But you must respect the fact that they are progressing and allow it. I view it as similar to when your child goes away to college and, as much as it tears at you, you know you have to trust and let them go; knowing that there will be a time when you will be united again. This is a wonderful lesson of faith, trust, and unconditional love. If, for some reason, you feel an incredibly strong urge to connect with a loved one who has passed on and cannot shake it off, then is the time to seek out a reputable Spiritist to help you to determine whether you should make that connection or seek some professional assistance in helping you to deal with the loss. [Note* A reputable Spiritist will turn you away if they feel that it is you and not the loved one who desires the connection during the loved one's transition time, better known as sleep state] An easy way to relieve some stress is to give up trying to control someone else's life. One of the most important factors to remember is that we are all individuals. And your life lessons vary both in the spiritual and the physical planes. This is one of the explanations for the many religions on the planet today. Each religion serves the needs and requirements for the spiritual path the member of that sect is on. When it no longer serves them, you will find that they will move on. One of the most tempting things we humans experience is the desire to judge and criticize others because they do not believe the same religious doctrines as we do. When you can allow another person their right of choice to walk the path they choose, without damning or criticizing them, you are definitely closer to the enlightened state. This does not mean neglect your children or that you should not offer them guidance, and gentle suggestions that you feel may enhance the quality of their life but, if they don't choose to accept them, it is important to respect that fact and allow them their right of choice. For only that individual's spirit knows truly the lessons their lifetime requires. This can be a difficult thing if your child or loved one has committed a criminal offense. But, if you have given them the proper guidance as a parent or guardian and done all you should or could do for them in that area and they still opt to be criminal in nature, then you should not feel guilty or stressed about it, since it is obviously something that is necessary for their growth process and not simply a mistake on your part. Being able to accept someone for who they are and live and let

live is a wonderful way to release stress in your life.

I placed this in this section because too many people fall into the belief trap that their deceased grandma or grandpa is watching over them and judging them for keeping up with the times and raising the children differently. Ever heard the saying "Grandma would turn in her grave if she knew"? Trust me... grandma has better things to do than criticize you and hang onto old fashioned ways.

UNDERSTANDING COLORS

SCIENTISTS ARE DISCOVERING that colors have a profound influence on our bodies, moods, thoughts, behaviors, and generations. You may not consciously realize it, but even you have some inkling about color and its effect on your behavioral pattern. How often have you stated, "I feel sad and blue today" or "She's looking at the world through rose colored glasses"

Many ancient civilizations believed that colors held magic powers for healing and communicating. Color was used as a prescription in illness (both mental and physical injuries), growing crops, when killing animals for food, deaths, and spiritual-ritualistic ceremonies.

I use color light during many of my healing sessions. Color, like beauty, seems to exist in the eye of the beholder. It is unique with each individual and is never perceived in exactly the same way. Your eyes give you the external sight of your environment and your mind's eye gives you the vision of your inner environment. It is important to remember that vision and sight are not the same and therefore should not be considered synonymous. It is not just your eyes that control your perception of color. It is your brain as well.

When the Polaroid camera was invented, this fact was taken into consideration. They studied how a photograph, when taken in a light that is reddish in glow from the tungsten lamp, would show the objects colored only in the red hue, but when the same object with human eyes, the colors were all there. This is because your eyes and brain work in unison to create the true color inside your head, which is something the film, at that time, could not do. The phenomena known as vision occurs when your vision synthesizes the missing colors in your visual cortex, and you perceive them.

Your responses to colors are automatic. An excellent example would be the reactions of a male when he sees the noticeable reddening of a female's lips, caused by the increased blood pressure from aroused emotions. In most cases, isn't he flirtatious? Perhaps this explains the wide spread use of red lipstick by women, from as far back as the time of the Egyptian Pharaohs.

Businesses have been known to pay millions of dollars to psychologists for research to discover which colors will prompt you to buy their products. Red and yellow have become the most popular packaging colors. Perhaps because these colors give the illusion of the package being bigger than it is and the colors can be associated with sunlight and fire. Personal shoppers and decorators, who are trained in the use of color, make comfortable incomes by assisting people with the right colors for them either in clothing or their homes.

Colors promote emotions. In a number of tests, violent people were placed in pink rooms and the results showed that a particular pink color had the power to tranquilize and replace aggressive impulses with passive ones. It has been noted that pink rooms seem to induce a long-term change in people who are exposed to them over a period of time. More testing showed that even a brief exposure to a room that was colored in pink could cause the muscles in your body to weaken to a certain extent for as long as 30 minutes. (Perhaps the reason why an acupuncturist I visited had an office in pink!) Interestingly, the color blue has been found to counteract this effect within a matter of a few seconds. Even more interesting is the discovery that pink colored rooms have the same tranquilizing effect on color-blind people who are actually unable to see the color pink.

Laboratory mice that have been raised under a rainbow of colors have shown that different colors caused the organs of their bodies to grow at different rates. Mice living under green lighting proved to be the least active, while those living under red lighting were the most active. People, likewise, are influenced by exposure to colors. Not surprisingly, the color red makes people perceive their environment as warmer than it actually is when the temperature is measured by a thermometer. It has been noted that people who work under the red illumination tend to react more quickly than those who are not, but their efficiency in performing tasks is lessened. It is my understanding that scientists have determined that red lighting can alter normal electrical patterns of the brain. Even brief exposure to the color red, can cause an immediate change in the way electricity travels through human skin.

Keeping the fact that colors vibrate in mind, think about how they vibrate and interact with the energies around them and utilize the laws of manifestation. A color vibration can promote harmony and tranquility or tenseness and unrest. You can use colors for effects in practically all situations in your life. You can influence an emotion in a room by way of design, the emotions you or others you meet feel and react by your clothing, manifestation with the use of candles, or healing with light therapy. (The thought vibration projected and mixed with the color vibration is often used in prayer treatments and manifestations.)

Since color is a wonderful way to ease stress, it is a good idea to keep a few colored lights on hand when a session is needed. When performing color light healing on yourself, each application of color should be for thirty minutes or more. It is always best not to exceed an hour at a time. Give your body a day's time to adjust and make the necessary changes and then, if need be, continue the exposure for another thirty to sixty minutes. It is a good idea to understand the basic colors and their suggested uses. Color light treatments can be performed at any time prior to a meal, but because it can influence the flow of energy, it is a good idea to wait a few hours after you have eaten. If you happen to get indigestion during a healing session, use the color yellow to help alleviate it.

Here is a list of some basic colors and their use:

Red: It has the lowest rate of vibration. Treating with this color stimulates your automatic nervous and circulatory systems. Red will stimulate and build the red corpuscles in your liver, which are stored in your bone. It also acts as a detoxifying agent. Red symbolizes sexual love, power, and the attainment of ambitions. It is the expressions of the primal life force. If you are performing a manifestation and burning a candle in a ritual, you would burn a red candle when you want to add intensity to the manifestation.

Orange: Increases oxygen by stimulating

your lungs and thyroid glands. It depresses your parathyroid glands. Orange stimulates the production of milk in mammary glands for nursing mothers. It can be used to relieve gas in digestive systems and alleviate convulsions and cramps in all parts of your body and is very effective for hiccups. Orange will decrease menstrual cramps and increase the discharges. If you have a boil, carbuncle or abscess, orange will help to draw it to a head. Please note: In rare situations, orange has been reported to induce vomiting when used for indigestion. Orange is a symbol of joy and creativity. It can be used to stimulate spiritual attainment. Orange can help to attract people, animals, and other things you may want in your life. When manifesting or praying for work, orange candles really help.

Yellow: Yellow depresses your spleen and your parathyroid gland. It increases your appetite and aids in better assimilation for better nutrition. (This makes it an ideal color for kitchens or dishes) Yellow will stimulate your lymphatic glands and act as a stimulant for many sluggish organs. Yellow is also a nerve stimulant and builder. It strengthens your heart for better circulation. Yellow will also kick your liver and gallbladder into gear for better elimination. Since insects and worms shy away from the color yellow, it is a great aid in destroying worms and driving them out of your body. Yellow stimulates and builds up your pancreas and helps loosen and aid in elimination of lime deposits that can cause arthritis. Yellow is the color of the flame of the candle with which you meditate and pray. In it you can learn to see the fulfillment of your desires. It can assist you in understanding and stimulating your dream activity.

Lemon: A variation of the color yellow, lemon will loosen, relax, and stimulate your elimination process. It will build and stimulate your brain for clearer and more positive thinking, loosen and eliminate mucus throughout your entire body and activate and loosen congestion in your colon. Lemon will help loosen and eliminate calcium deposits and will activate your thymus gland (which is great if you are seeking more rapid growth in growth retarded children) Lemon will heal broken bones faster and will help soften hardened bones. It is extremely effective in eliminating the common cold. Lemon color, when used in prayer and manifestation will pull in Divine manifestation energy.

Green: Green is a primary healing color and should Green: always be used in conjunction with whatever other color you are using. The vibration from the color green will help your body receive the other colors with more effective results. Green stimulates your pituitary gland. It will also stimulate your immune system. Green is the standard color for all disorders of either chronic or acute conditions. In most cases, it dissolves blood clots in any part of your body in less than an hour. Green will help ease open sores and bruises and is a powerful combatant for cancer cells. Green promotes movement and growth and balances the energies of your body and mind. Green can stimulate health, greater abundance, increase fertility and promote youthfulness. When used in meditation, it can help open levels of consciousness, which are aware of the nature of the spirits in your

life.

White: White is the symbol of purity and power. It is the universal color that amplifies the effects of any other color being used with it or it can be used alone. It promotes cleansing and awakens hope. White can be used to initiate new energy movement in manifestation. When you are burning a white candle (unless the candle is of extremely poor quality) and it smokes, it indicates that the negativity in the area is being burned away.

Blue: Blue, when combined with red, will increase perspiration as a fever is broken. Blue increases vitality yet produces a peaceful effect for a more sound sleep. It relieves irritations and itching as well as fevers and burns and is powerful healing for children. Blue is the symbol of spiritual understanding and communication. It awakens your innate abilities to perceive. It is also a symbol of life and it alerts within your consciousness a greater faith in the life process. Blue candles have been known to be burned in various rituals to bring in quick money.

Black: Black is a very powerful color. It is also one of the most protective (and most misunderstood). It can be used to bring a person back down to earth since it is an excellent grounding color. It can also be used in various rituals to uncover secrets and for understanding the purposes of actions we have made. Black can be used in meditation to help us find the light within the dark. It stabilizes and awakens greater responsibility. It is most effective in candle burning, when burned with a white candle. Please use caution with black since an abundance of it can actually manifest negativity.

Violet: Violet has the shortest wavelength of the visible colors. It depresses all over-active parts of your body with the exception of your spleen and parathyroid. It relaxes and calms your nerves and is also an antibiotic. Violet stimulates and builds the white corpuscles in your spleen. Violet will help with weight reduction by depressing your appetite and working on your lymphatic system. Violet also gives relief from diarrhea. Violet is the symbol of spirituality, power, and mastery. It will awaken success, elevation, and attainment of spiritual desires. Burning a violet or purple candle during meditation will assist in opening your third eye.

Pink: Pink will raise or lower your blood pressure in accordance to what your body needs. It

stimulates your heart and assists your veins and arteries to function normally. Pink also aids in the function of your kidneys and adrenal gland and will balance your sexual desires and activities. Since pink is a "balancing" color, it can be used for all illnesses. Pink is a symbol of love and success. It awakens a consciousness of clean living and honor. It stimulates purity of intention and it can bring forth a vision of truth and success. Burning a pink candle during a meditation or prayer enhances these vibrations.

Gray: Although not used for healing your body in light therapy, gray is a symbol of clarity and balance. You can meditate with a gray candle to see how best to initiate new activities. It awakens that level of the subconscious mind that is aware of how the wheels of life are turning for you. Gray candles are burned when studying astrology to help in understanding the planetary in-fluences. Gray awakens your most innate primal intuition.

Brown: Although not used for healing your body in light therapy, brown is a neutral color. It is grounding and can awaken a greater discernment and more certainty. The color brown candle can be used when meditating to find or uncover lost articles. It is the color associated with St. Jude, the patron of lost causes. Even though my primary focus has been on using colors for light therapy and in manifestation and prayer, keep in mind that the colors you wear on a daily basis will also have an effect on you and the people you come in contact with. Therefore, select your wardrobe wisely each morning to add to your success throughout the day.

STONES

AS WITH EVERYTHING on this planet, the rate of vibration and the compatibility of that vibration with the energy flowing through it will determine the usage and affect the innate object plays in your reality.

Although they do not have a life force of their own, stones do afford an amplifying effect on the energy you are working with. So, when you are feeling excess stress, you can amplify the vibration you have chosen to work with to assist you in relieving that stress with a stone. When I think about them, I look at them as a type of magnifying glass, enhancing, and enlarging what is being directed through it.

As we have discussed in previous chapters, you have the inherent ability to create on your own, just by thought. It is not necessary to use objects for creating, but many people prefer the assistance of objects or tools.

You can wear stones in the form of jewelry. You will most often see me with a blue topaz ring and bracelet, a gold bracelet, neck chain and earrings and a diamond ring. All have a specific healing purpose as well as making great body decoration. Diamonds are a powerful amplifier, as well as a beautiful piece of jewelry! You can place a stone in with your houseplant to assist it with its growth. Or you can lay a stone over a chakra (or even wear it) to help attract the necessary or desired vibration ray, or place it over a part of your body that may need help with amplifying healing energies. You can place stones in the four-corners of your home for balance and harmony or treat your drinking water by placing a stone in the bottom of the pitcher being used. To pull the protective vibration energies to you while you are sleeping, place them under your mattress. As you can see there are many wonderful uses for stones of all colors.

The following is a list of the most popular stones and their property uses as told to me from varying sources. You can find most of them at any "World of Science" store.

Agate: Variety of types;

Blue Lace Agate: Reduces quarrels, brings peace and harmony to the environment

Banded Agate: Protections, promotes body energy.

Botswana Agate: Use against depression and stress.

Leopard skin Agate: Safe astral travel.

Moss Agate: Connect to the earth and Mother Nature.

Turritella Agate: Past life regression.

Yellowstone River Agate: Muscle cramps, aches.

Zebra Agate: Guards against physical damage. Angelite: Promotes peace and comfort, puts you in touch with your guardian spirits, anti- nightmare.

Aragonite: Insight, wisdom, helps to see the truth. Apatite: Communication, healing, creativity, and aids in weight loss.

Apache Tear: Wards off negativity, protection stone, releases past emotional hurts.

Amazonite: Business success, draws money

Amber: Eating disorders, gracefulness, astral projection, past life regression

Amethyst: Alcohol recovery, psychism, dreams, meditation, opens third eye

Aventurine: Aids eyesight, money, luck, healing

Azurite: Insight, dreams, healing, communication Ametrine: Meditation, attunement, reach a higher state more quickly.

Apophyllite: Connects physical to spiritual, helps you to realize your own behavior.

Aquamarine: Communication, purification

Beryl: Healing love, repels gossip, promotes clarity

Bloodstone: Circulation

Baoji: Balances and expands your energy

Carnelian: Female reproductive system; eases cramps and muscle aches

Calcite: Variety of types;

Blue Calcite: Healing, creativity, and communication

Green Calcite: Money, luck, calms your heart

Honey Calcite: Spinal and back aches, reduces pain

Optical Calcite: Memory

Orange Calcite: Strength, female reproductive system

Pink Calcite: Calms, grounds, centers, promotes love

Red Calcite: Desire, passion, increased sex drive

Celestite: Attracts spirits, calming effect on the soul

Charoite: Connects the heart and the crown chakras. Chrysocolla: Promotes wisdom

Chrysoprase: Luck, success, protection, and friendship

Citrine: Promotes psychic energy

Copper: Conductive properties strengthen the influence of other stones

Coal: Draws money

Danburite: Enhances your aura

Desert Rose: Lactose tolerance, aids breast milk

Dolomite: Relieves sorrow and grief

Emerald: Successful love, money

Enhydro: Healing

Flint: Telepathy

Fossil: Past life regressions

Fluorite: Variety of types;

Blue Fluorite: Calming energy

Chinese Fluorite: Protects against disease, healing Green Fluorite: cleanses negativity

Purple Fluorite: Open's your third eye, promotes intuition

Yellow Fluorite: Intellect, will- power

Fuchsite: reveals the truth

Garnet: Sexual energy

Geode: Promotes connection with inner self

Halite: purification, cleansing, healing Hematite: Grounding

Quartz: Variety of types;

Aqua Aura Quartz: Transformation and manifestation

Blue Phantom Quartz: Spiritual connection

Clear Quartz: Universal stone, when in doubt... use clear quartz

Golden Healer Quarts: Healing on all levels

Herkimer Diamond: Enhances awareness

Lavender Rose Quartz: Promotes clairvoyance and clairaudience

Rainbow Quartz: Used to stimulate all of the chakras Record Keeper Quartz: Retains information until it is channeled out. It is associated with the lost continents of Lemuria and Atlantis.

Rose Quartz: Love

Rutilated Quartz: Psychic ability

Smokey Quartz: Relieves stress, helps with mood swings and sleeplessness

Tourmelated Quartz: Protects against negative energy Window Quartz: Reflection of self-image

Rhodochrosite: Physical energy

Rhondonite: Releases confusion

Ruby: Wealth, sexual energy, love, joy

Sandstone: Weight issues

Sodalite: Overall healing

Sugilite: Psychic enhancement draws to you the angels or spirit guides

Selenite: Lactose intolerance, breast milk

Soapstone: Calming effect

Spectrolite: Awakens creativity

Stibnite: Enhances energy

Sulphur: Healing

Sunstone: Clears and energizes chakras

Talc: Soothes anger

Tektite: Connects you with guides and spiritual teachers

Tiger's Eye: Variety of types;

Black Tigers Eye: Wards off negativity

Blue Tigers Eye: Promotes creativity

Gold Tigers Eye: Money

Multi Tigers Eye: Divination protection

Red Tigers Eye: Strengthens body force

Topaz, Blue: Healing

Topaz, White: Love

Tourmaline: Variety of Types:

Black Tourmaline: Wards off negativity

Blue Tourmaline: Communication

Colorless Tourmaline: Calms and soothes

Green Tourmaline: Business success

Pink Tourmaline: Promotes love and friendship

Watermelon Tourmaline: Draws love energy

Trilobite: Leadership, strength, and patience

Turquoise: Healing, protection
Ulexite: Psychic intuition and healing
Unakite: calms emotions
Wulfenite: Transition from physical plane to psychic plane: astral traveling
Zeolite: Clears toxins
Zincate: Removes energy blockages

DEVELOPING YOUR SIXTH SENSE

DEVELOPING YOUR SIXTH sense is another excellent means of stress management. I recall how much more relaxed and comfortable I became once I began to understand and learn to work with, instead of against, my own abilities. Although everyone has access to the sixth sense, confusion lies as to exactly what it is and also, to what degree you have it. In my earlier days of psychic development, I often heard individuals referring to their "sixth sense" and when I asked what that meant, I was given mixed explanations. (Including that use of them was demonic!) I believe that is because we all have different abilities that are prominent to us and these abilities are governed by our belief systems. Therefore, one individual may view the sixth sense as the sense of insight, while another views it as the sense of touch. Both are correct. It is my understanding that the sixth sense or should I say, senses, are those that are of the non-physical mixing with the physical. For example, you may sense the nausea another person is experiencing, or you could go beyond that sense and experience the nausea within your own physical body. This is what is meant by being empathic. Another individual may sense the foul odor of something being described or go even further and not only sense what it smells like, but actually experience the odor.

Getting in tune with your own body and recognizing the stronger factors of intuition is the first step to developing your own sixth sense. The easiest way to accomplish this is through meditation. When you allow yourself to relax and feel what is going on within your body, you will become so familiar with it that when a sensation occurs that is not what you would consider "normal" to you, you will be able to determine whether it is discord in your body due to dis-ease or due to external influences. [i.e. the sixth sense.] If you are serious about developing your sixth sense, I recommend spending a minimum of 20 minutes per day focusing only on feeling what is happening within your body, for the first week. After that, you should begin to feel the energies around you when you are out of meditation. For example, when you are out in public, try to feel the sensations being projected from the people around you; are they happy? Are they sad? Are they ill? Are they healthy? Once you have determined that you feel the energy they are projecting, watch their body language for signs of validation, or better yet, strike up a conversation with them. A person's attitude or health often shows up in their tone of voice or usage of words.

Your first try should be in a relaxing environment, such as a library or a bookstore, then work your way up to a grocery store. I don't suggest going to a nightclub environment in the beginning, since the vibrations are filled, for the most part, with masses of negativity.

Understanding the universal laws and accepting them to be true will allow you to comfortably open up to your own inherent senses. When you are able to determine the type of sensations a person's projecting, the next step is to trust your intuition on a deeper level. Trust your instincts. The following exercises will help you to trust your senses and develop them to optimum. They are important tools in development. Once you have mastered these, you are ready for the next step in feeling good and relieving stress.

Exercise One: Sensing Your Physical Surroundings:

Find a location that is crowded but not congested with too much activity, such as a warehouse or an inactive parking lot. Keeping your eyes tightly closed, begin walking, using your senses to visualize or feel what is before you. Take your time. If you sense or see something in front of you with your third eye, stop and open your eyes for validation then close them and continue. The primary goal is to be able to walk the length of the area without bumping into anything, while keeping your eyes closed. Someone who has lost their vision has already mastered the uses of these senses.

*Note: I suggest that you don't blindfold yourself, since you may need to open your eyes

quickly for safety purposes.

Exercise Two: Developing your inner eye:

It is possible to do this on your own, but much more fun when you have someone joining you. It can actually become a great party game!

Take an ordinary deck of playing cards. In the beginning, make a selection of 5 cards and remove them from the deck. Using these cards only, lay them face down. Have someone select a card from the selection and hold it up, not showing you what it is. (If you are alone doing this exercise, simply separate a selected card from the others without looking at it). Center yourself and concentrate on the card. The goal here is to know which card they (you) are holding from the ones you have separated from the deck. You will either see it with your third eye, [i.e. envision it in your mind] or you will have a sense of what it is, or you may actually hear the name of the card in your head. Any of these is fine, as long as you come up with the correct answer. This takes a lot of practice and the key is to not get frustrated. Allow yourself to relax and perceive to the best of your ability. Once you have become fairly successful with selecting the correct one out of the few you have separated from the deck, make it more challenging until you are able to do it from the entire deck! You can also use flash cards etc., for this exercise.

Exercise Three: Automatic Writing:

The spiritual and angelic realm can be a marvelous help when you are working on healing yourself, either emotionally or physically, or both! They will guide you as to where the core of the situation is and prompt you as to the correct movement to shift the energies. Feeling comfortable with your connection is important. Meditation, of course, is my primary recommended method of connecting with both the spiritual and angelic realm. You can also just pray and trust the urges you receive after you have done a prayer request. Another excellent way to receive guidance and information from the spiritual and angelic realm is through the process of automatic writing. It is important that you surround yourself with protective Christ energy or white light before beginning automatic writing. Since it is a form of channeling; you will need protection in order to not be vulnerable to the negativity. (See meditation) Positioning yourself comfortably with a pen and paper, place yourself in a relaxed state of consciousness. Do not try to control the pen in your hand, just allow it to flow. When thoughts pop up in your mind, write them down immediately without trying to make sense of them or to create any story, just write them down. You will find, as you keep your mind relaxed and just write the thoughts out there will be wonderful messages from the spiritual or angelic realm. I recommend keeping a journal of your writings. Those that seem to be meaningless at the time of receiving them often make sense when looking back.

YOUR BODY AND ITS CARE

THE COMMON MISCONCEPTION of people is that we are a spirit with a physical body and that is all. You actually have a total of seven bodies. The one you are aware of is your physical body. But there is also your etheric body, your astral body, your mental body, your emotional body, your spiritual body, and your soul body. The health and balance of all of these bodies needs to be taken into consideration in order to have optimum health.

Your physical body is the one you are aware of. It is the final result of the condensing and densifying of vibrations. Your physical body responds and reacts to the prompting of your other bodies, either in a positive or a negative manner. When there is dis-ease in one or more of your bodies, if allowed to linger for an extended period of time, it will eventually condense to disease. Various parts of our physical body are directly linked to your other bodies.

Your etheric body is the energy field around you; most commonly referred to as your aura. This field of energy or body is the median between your physical body and your other bodies. Manifestations enter and leave your physical body by way of your etheric body. Cleansing of your etheric body is just as important as cleansing your physical body, if not more so, since it hold energies from both directions. All chakras are associated with your etheric body.

Your astral body takes charge when you are in an altered or sleep state. It is always busy, traveling through time and space gathering information and learning. Your astral body is your connection between the worlds. It is not uncommon to do "astral travel-ing" when you are sleeping, in meditation or in a light trance. Your astral body is the busy beaver of your bodies. The chakras associated with your astral body are the 3rd, 4th, 5th, 6th, and 7th chakras (or vortexes).

Your mental body is the thinker of the group, as states the name. Keeping your mental body balanced and free of negative thoughts is the first step to complete and whole health. Positive affirmations and prayer are excellent ways to cleanse your mental body. The primary chakra associated with your mental body is the 6th chakra, commonly referred to as your third eye.

Your emotional body is your sensitive body. It collects and gathers emotions and feelings. It is very important to keep your emotional body balanced to avoid illness. Your emotional body interacts equally with all your bodies and acts as a filter for vibrations. When you allow your emotional body to be cluttered and imbalanced, it becomes a breeding ground for dis-ease. The primary chakra for your emotional body is your third chakra, also called your solar plexus.

Your soul body is your core. It houses all the memories of all that you have experienced and encountered. It knows the real you, and releases facets of you during each incarnation in accordance to the lesson plan for that particular life. Your soul body will recognize it is compatible companion from the same "over-soul" (equate it to a human mother) and draw you to that person. Your soul body is connected to all the chakras.

Your spiritual body is your body that

connects you with the divine. It is the exact duplicate of your physical body. Your spiritual body enables you to stay in touch with the multi dimensions, interacting and communicating with them in accordance to your developed skills. It is your one body that lives on eternally. The spiritual body is most closely associated with your crown chakra.

Your first six bodies are maintained primarily through chakra balancing, meditation, and prayer. Colors and scents can also help with their vibration regulations. Your physical body needs a little more attention. By using the tools Infinite Creator put on the planet, (I.E. foods and herbs), you can provide a balanced maintenance plan and reduce, if not eliminate trips to the doctor. It is important to remember that your physical body is sixty-six percent water; so, although I am discussing foods and herbs, do not forget to drink sufficient pure water to supplement your needs. The average person loses about a quart of water per day through perspiration, urination, etc. You need to replace at least that with pure, filtered drinking water. I recommend avoiding plastic bottled water, since the water itself has a very limited shelf life and the source is not always closely monitored. Not to mention the toxins from the plastic container.

Mineral water, purified water, or reversed osmosis water in a glass container is your purest drinking element.

There's a saying: "You are what you eat," and it could not be truer. Think about the last time you had a headache, or a stomach ache, or felt cranky, or bloated. How about your complexion? Is it peaches and cream? Or is it showing signs of stress? Although your body requires a certain amount of exercise to keep it healthy, true health starts inside. It starts with nutrition.

A healthy body does not always mean a size "4" body! We are all made differently in the eyes of Infinite Creator and not all of us are meant to be a skinny as modern-day actresses or models. There are some very healthy bodies at a size that might be considered too large in accordance to the standards of today's society (I say today, because it was not always the case through history). Please consult your physician and not your local "body guru" for an idea of what size is right and perfect for your

particular body type.

The following are some of the basic foods and their health/healing properties. Once you have identified their benefits to your body, you will never look at dinner in the same manner again!

[*Most commonly used are listed first.]

(Flavorings)

Garlic: Garlic helps you manage your blood cholesterol by pushing down levels of LDL (bad cholesterol) and raising levels of HDL (good cholesterol); it has antioxidant properties that help prevent the buildup of plaque in your arteries. It lowers blood pressure, is a natural antibiotic, and a powerful cancer fighter.

Possible side effects: Some people have a sensitivity to garlic and cannot use it in large amounts without feeling nauseous and hot. Other people may develop gas and bloating as a result of not being able to digest its sulfur compounds well. For people with sensitive skin, garlic can create an

irritation.

Onion: In raw form an onion, like garlic helps you manage your cholesterol by pushing down levels of LDL (bad cholesterol) and raising levels of HDL (good cholesterol). It helps to prevent blood clots by keeping platelets from sticking together and dissolving clots that have already formed. Onion enhances the effectiveness of insulin activity to help lower blood sugar levels. It helps with allergies - hay fever -asthma; the quercetin in an onion acts as a mild sedative to help you sleep. Green onions and chives (with the green tops) are a good source of vitamin A.

Possible side effects: Some people have a sensitivity to onion and cannot use it in large amounts without feeling nauseous and hot. Other people may develop gas and bloating as a result of not being able to digest its sulfur compounds well.

Cinnamon: Cinnamon has a germicidal effect, making it an excellent blood cleaner. When it is used in a mouthwash; it can help fight infections. It stops gas in the stomach in small amounts and will act as a laxative in larger amounts.

Possible side effects: In rare cases cinnamon may elevate blood pressure. If you are prone to or already have high blood pressure consult with your doctor or Naturopath before using it on a daily basis. Since it has a laxative effect, if you have a stomach virus or the flu, it could worsen the situation.

Clove: Clove has antiseptic properties making it an effective blood cleanser. It has a mild numbing effect making it great for temporary relief of toothaches. It will freshen your breath when you chew on it.

Possible side effects: Clove could create a burning sensation in your mouth and stomach if overused.

Cayenne: Cayenne is useful in alleviating debilitating arthritis pain. (Capsaicin, as the active ingredient is known, is even a main ingredient in expensive over the-counter and prescription pain medications.) Cayenne has a use for treating the following: arthritis, backache, bunions, heart disease, ulcers, carpal tunnel, emphysema, fever, herpes, indigestion, pain, psoriasis, shingles, and there is more. Notice a common link? They all can benefit from improved circulation and endorphin production.

Possible Side Effects: Cayenne could create a burning sensation in your stomach and acid reflux in certain individuals

Cardamom: Cardamom assists with clearer breathing with asthma and allergy attacks. It helps maintain your lungs and aids in soothing your digestive tract and nervous system, as well aid in sleeping.

Possible side effects: I am not aware of any.

Ginger: Ginger can aid in improving pain, stiffness, mobility and swelling. It can be used to help reduce nausea, reduces gas, bloating and indigestion and aids in your body's use and absorption of other nutrients and medicines. It is also a valuable deterrent to intestinal worms, particularly roundworms. Used topically, ginger stimulates circulation in your skin as well as underlying tissues. You can use a ginger root poultice on your chest for lung congestion or on your abdomen for gas and nausea.

Possible side effects: Since ginger can warm and raise body temperature slightly, it should be avoided when this is undesired, such as in the case of menopausal hot flashes.

Horseradish: Horseradish is helpful for sinus infections. It also increases facial circulation and promotes expulsion of mucus from upper respiratory passages. Horseradish has mild antibiotic effects and can stimulate urine production, thus helping with urinary tract infections. When used topically, it can help with pain of arthritis and nerve irritation. A horseradish poultice can be used to treat infected wounds.

Possible Side Effects: Pain in your head, especially behind the root of your nose can occur. Large, repetitive doses of horseradish may cause stomach upset and even vomiting in some people. It may be especially irritating if you are already suffering indigestion from eating cruciferous vegetables, such as cabbage or broccoli. When used as a poultice, horseradish may redden your skin and cause a rash.

Myrrh: Myrrh can be used as an antiseptic and preservative. Modern research has shown that it stimulates the production of white blood cells, boosts your immune system and is an excellent way to promote oral health. Mouthwashes and toothpaste found in natural health stores often contain myrrh as an active ingredient. Mixed with other ingredients, it can be a potent topical antiseptic salve. Myrrh has been found to fight gum disease, is recommended as a gargle in cases of mumps, and helps fight tooth decay.

Possible side effects: I am not aware of any.

Peppermint: Peppermint is commonly used to relieve gas, nausea, and stomach pain due to irritable bowel, intestinal cramps, or indigestion. It also has analgesic, antiseptic, antispasmodic with decongestant and cooling properties. When used topically it has a cooling, relaxing effect as well as aids with relief of itching.

Possible side effects: Peppermint could have a reverse effect on some people and cause headaches, stomach upset and skin rashes.

Saffron: In traditional Indian medicine (Ayurveda), saffron is used as an aphrodisiac, a cure for arthritis, asthma, to reduce a fever, healing your liver and combating alcoholism. It is thought that an active ingredient in saffron can lower blood cholesterol as well.

Possible side effects: I am not aware of any.

Sage: Sage aids in digestion and can stimulate your appetite. Sage is reported to have an estrogenic as well as a cooling action. It has been used to assist in lessening excessive uterine bleeding and for cramps that feel worse with heat applications and better with cold applications. It helps in stopping breast milk production and can be helpful with treating diarrhea, colds, and excessive perspiration. Sage can dry up phlegm and when used as a gargle can be helpful with tonsil and throat infections. Because of its antibiotic properties, when used in a hair rinse, it can help

with the treatment of dandruff.

Possible side effects: I am not aware of any.

(Fruits)

Apples: Apples have mild anti-viral and antibacterial properties. They help prevent inflammation, assist in treating constipation, and regulate blood sugar levels. Apples also help lover your cholesterol levels.

Apricots: Apricots help prevent heart disease, cataracts, and many types of cancer. They are a very good source of vitamin C.

Avocado: The fat in an avocado is the same heart healthy mono-unsaturated fat found in olive oil. They also help to fight cancer and prevent cataracts. Avocados are a good source of potassium and magnesium.

Bananas: Bananas are non-allergenic, soothe an upset stomach and help to fight ulcers. They are an excellent source of potassium, magnesium and B6. Bananas interact with female hormones to alleviate symptoms of pre-menstrual syndrome (PMS).

Blueberries: Blueberries help to alleviate bladder infect-ions, and diarrhea or irritable bowel syndrome. They also contain phytochemicals that slow down vision loss associated with age.

Cranberries: Cranberries help to alleviate urinary tract infections. Contrary to belief, cranberries do not possess as much potassium and vitamins as blueberries.

Dates: Dates are an excellent source of fiber, potassium, and boron. They help post-menopausal women avoid heart disease and osteoporosis. Dates are a natural form of aspirin and may help alleviate pain as well as prevent strokes.

Please note: Dates contain amines, chemicals that can trigger headaches in certain people.

Grapes: Grapes help to fight cancer, lower your cholesterol, and prevent heart disease. They contain boron, a mineral linked to bone health and also encourages your body to make estrogen, thus mimicking hormone replacement therapy in post-menopausal women. Grapes help fight osteoporosis.

Grapefruit: Grapefruit is an excellent source of vitamin C and is high in cancer fighting agents. Grapefruit also helps to lower your blood cholesterol.

Guava: Guava's high in fiber. It helps to prevent prostate cancer. Guava is a rich source of Vitamin C and potassium and helps lower cholesterol and blood pressure levels.

Kiwifruit: Kiwifruit has more vitamin C than in an orange and almost as much fiber as in a cup of bran flakes. Kiwifruit fights cancer, heart disease, and cataracts, plus helps to stabilize blood sugar levels. It is an excellent source of potassium.

Melons: Melons help prevent blood clots. They are an excellent source of potassium and vitamin A. Certain melons contain mild antibacterial sub-stances.

Mangos: Mangos are a superior source of vitamin A and C. They also contain several B vitamins potassium, calcium, and magnesium and
are high in fiber.

Orange: The orange is a great source of vitamin C, and potassium. It fights cancer and is high in fiber plus contains a small amount of calcium.

Papaya: Papaya has more Vitamin C than an orange. It helps to fight cancer, cataracts, and heart disease. Papaya is an excellent source of potassium.

Pineapple: Pineapple contains manganese (bone strengthening mineral), copper, thiamin and vitamin C. Pineapple helps prevent osteoporosis, lighten heavy menstrual flow and aids in digestion.

Raisins: Raisins are high in fiber, potassium, and boron. They help fight colon cancer, and lower blood cancer. Raisins also assist in lowering cravings for nicotine.

Please Note: Raisins contain a lot of amines, which are chemical substances that can trigger headaches in some people.

Tomatoes: Tomatoes are high in Vitamin A, C and Potassium. They help to lower your blood cholesterol and fight heart disease.

(Vegetables)

Asparagus: Asparagus is a good source of Vitamins A, C, folate, and potassium. It helps to prevent cataracts, cancer and lowers blood pressure.

Beet Greens: Beet Greens raise the alkaline in your body, thus reducing any craving for nicotine.

They are an excellent source of vitamin A, C, potassium, and folate. Beet greens help to keep your kidneys and lungs healthy.

Beet Root: Beet Root cleans your liver and is

high in folate, potassium and fiber, fights cancer, lowers cholesterol and regulates intestinal tract and blood sugar.

Broccoli: Broccoli is a good source of vitamin A, C, folate, lutein, chromium, calcium, and fiber. It is a powerful cancer fighter as well as bacteria fighter. Broccoli stabilizes blood sugar levels.

Cabbage: Cabbage kills ulcer causing bacteria when raw and lowers risks of estrogen related cancers. Cabbage helps prevent osteoporosis and regulates blood pressure. It is a good source of fiber, calcium, vitamin A and vitamin C.

Carrots: Carrots are high in vitamin A and a good source of fiber. They are a powerful cancer fighter and help to keep your eyes healthy.

Cauliflower: Cauliflower is a natural cancer fighter, and most notably against breast and colon cancers. After citrus fruits, it is the next best source of vitamin C. Cauliflower is also a good source of potassium and fiber.

Celery: Celery helps to regulate your blood pressure.

Collard Greens: Collard Greens are an excellent source of vitamin A and lutein. They also help to fight cancer. Please note: Collard Greens are high in oxalates, which bind calcium into un-absorbable complexes. People who are prone to kidney stones should be careful not to eat too many collard greens.

Dandelion Greens: Dandelion Greens are very high in vitamin A, potassium, calcium, iron, thiamin, riboflavin, and antioxidants. They help prevent cancer and cataracts. Dandelion Greens also helps reduce cravings for nicotine.

Mushrooms: Mushrooms lower cholesterol and thin your blood. They are a potent immune system builder. Please note: Sadly, common button mushrooms have no known nutritional value and actually contain hydrazine, which are toxic compounds which leave when cooked. Although hydrazine has been found to cause tumors in animals, the extent of its threat to humans is unknown, never-the-less it is recommended that you limit your intake of raw button mushrooms and stick to shakti or other types.

Parsley: Parsley is high in most vitamins; a

small amount contains more folate than an orange and nearly a day's amount of vitamin C and A. Parsley's rich in calcium, potassium and antioxidants and makes a good diuretic.

Parsnip: Parsnips are high in fiber, folate, and potassium. Parsnip helps prevent cancer and keeps your colon healthy.

Peppers: All peppers are a good source of vitamin A and C but red peppers are also an excellent source of antioxidants. Green peppers have twice as much vitamin C as citrus fruit and red peppers have three times as much. Both hot and sweet peppers are excellent cancer fighting agent and help to heal ulcers

Potatoes: Potatoes contain most of the

vitamins with the exception of vitamin A. They are high in fiber, iron, potassium, and copper. Potatoes help to regulate your blood pressure and serotonin levels. Please note: Potatoes have recently been identified as a potential culprit for irritable bowel syndrome.

Spinach: Spinach is high in vitamin A, , iron and calcium. It helps prevent cancer, heart disease and cataracts. Spinach builds your immune system and helps reduce nicotine cravings. Note: Spinach is a high oxalic food, which prevents the absorption of calcium and should be avoided by people who are prone to kidney stones.

Squash: Squash is high in antioxidants and potassium. It helps fight cancer and regulates your blood pressure.

Sweet Potatoes: Sweet Potatoes contain more beta-carotene than carrots. They help lower your cholesterol and reduce your risk of stroke. Sweet potatoes also help build your immune system. They are especially good for preventing colds and flu and

are an excellent source of potassium and vitamin C.

(Beverages)

Soy Milk: Soy Milk is rich in potassium and iron. It also helps regulate estrogen levels.

Green tea and **Oolong tea**: Green tea and Oolong tea help to prevent cancer, have anti-bacterial properties, lower cholesterol, protect your liver and contain a natural source of fluoride. They also contain manganese for healthy bones. Both can be used to treat diarrhea.

Wine: Red wines contain strong antioxidants. They help reduce heart disease, strokes cancer, cataracts, and other diseases of aging. White wines contain a lesser value but will do the same on a lesser scale.

(Salad Greens)

Iceberg, sometimes called head lettuce, is the most commonly used lettuce for salads and unfortunately has virtually no nutrients in it. It is wiser to get greens that can provide a boost to your body. The other greens and lettuces are filled with vitamins and minerals. So, by-pass the iceberg and build your salad with other greens.

(Vitamins)

A: An important "medicine" for the immune system, it keeps your skin and mucous membrane cells healthy, thus helping them to resist cell damage such as cancer. The moistness inhibits bacteria and viruses from taking hold. It also plays a major role in eye health. Vitamin A is quite plentiful in a large variety of fruits and vegetables.

B-1: Also known as Thiamin, it helps your body to manufacture less fats and metabolize protein as well as normalize the functioning of your nervous system. Thiamin is found naturally in pork, oysters, green peas, and lima beans.

B-2: Also called Riboflavin, B-2 helps metabolize carbohydrates, fats, and proteins for energy. Riboflavin has a connection to glutathione, one of the enzymes that rid your body of free radicals. It helps in the regeneration of this beneficial compound. The single best source for B-2 is milk, but it can also be found in meats, especially liver and kidney and some green leafy vegetables.

B-3: Also known as Niacin, assists in the conversion of protein, carbohydrates, and fats into energy. The amino acid tryptophan can be converted by your body to niacin. Most proteins contain tryptophan and make a good source for niacin. Certain mushrooms and greens are also a good source.

B-5: Also called Pantothenic Acid, it helps release energy from carbo-hydrates, fats, and proteins. It also helps in the metabolism of fats and the production of red blood cells and hormones from your adrenal gland. All foods contain B-5 in some amount, but the best sources include eggs, salmon, liver, kidney, peanuts, wheat bran and yeast.

B-6: Also called Pyridoxine mainly helps

metabolize protein and amino acids. Though not directly involved in the release of energy, like some of the other B vitamins, B-6 helps remove the nitrogen from amino acids, making them available as sources of energy. Because of its work with proteins, it plays a role in the synthesis of protein substances such as muscles, antibodies, and hormones. It also helps in the production of neurotransmitters (chemical messenger) and red blood cells. B6 is in all foods in one form or another but the best sources are meats, whole wheat, salmon, nuts, wheat germ, brown rice, peas, and beans.

B-12: Also called Cyano-cobalamin, it is essential to cells because it is needed to assist folate in making DNA and RNA, which carry and transmit genetic information for every living cell. B12 functions in the production of a material called myelin, which covers and protects nerve fibers. Without enough B12 the myelin sheath does not form properly or stay healthy and there can be irreversible damage that eventually ends in death.

Biotin: Another B vitamin, it functions in

the metabolism of fats and carbohydrates, in the breakdown of protein to urea, and the conversion of amino acids from protein into blood sugar for energy. Milk, liver, egg yolk, yeast and dried peas/beans are good sources of biotin. Nuts and certain mushrooms contain smaller amounts of biotin and bacteria in the intestinal tract can also make it.

C: Also known as Ascorbic Acid it is a major contributor in the formation and repair of collagen. It also promotes normal development of bones and teeth. Vitamin C is also needed for amino acid metabolism and synthesis of hormones, including thyroid hormones It is also an antioxidant and helps in cholesterol metabolism and immune functioning. It is a great cancer fighter. Citrus fruits are excellent sources of vitamin C, but it can also be found in potatoes, peppers, and other fresh vegetables. Overcooking of foods will destroy vitamin C.

C0-Q: A fat-soluble vitamin that stimulates your immune system, improve your heart health, heals periodontal disease, facilitates weight loss, boosts energy, and promotes general sense of well-being. It is present in many foods, especially organ meat, oily fish, and whole grains.

D-3: A vitamin also known as Cholecalciferol,

and can be made in your body, providing you get sufficient sunshine. It is necessary to help your body absorb the minerals calcium and phosphorus, which are needed for the proper growth and development of your bones and teeth. It also regulates whether these minerals are deposited into your bone or withdrawn out of your bone to meet other needs. Few foods contain a significant amount of vitamin D naturally and the ones that do are not ones you want to overeat, such as butter, cream, egg yolks and liver. All milk is fortified with vitamin D

E: Also known as Tocopherol, it functions as an antioxidant in your cells and tissues of your body. It protects lung cells that are in constant contact with oxygen and white blood cells that help fight disease. Vitamin E helps maintain a healthy immune system. Good sources are oils and margarine from corn, cottonseed, soy-bean, safflower, and wheat germ.

Folate: Another B vitamin, it plays an important role in making new cells because it helps form the genetic material DNA and RNA that carry and transmit the genetic information to for cell production. It helps in the production of your red blood cells. Green leafy vegetables, such as broccoli, spinach and asparagus are rich in folate. Seeds, liver and dried peas and beans are other good sources.

K: Vitamin K gets its name from the Danish word koagulation, meaning "coagulation" or "clotting." The proteins used in blood clotting require vitamin K. When there is not which can increase the amount of blood lost. Vitamin K also helps make a protein, called Osteocalcin, that binds calcium. It can be found in green leafy vegetables as well as beef liver, chicken liver, pork liver, milk, and eggs. Without sufficient k in your system, your blood takes longer to clot.

(Minerals)

Boron: A minerals that's main function is to help your body turn vitamin D into its most active form to regulate how much calcium is put into your bones or drawn out of them. Boron also has a beneficial effect on estrogen, which plays a role in your bone health. It can be found in soil rich fruits, vegetables, and nuts.

Calcium: The human body contains more calcium than any other mineral. Your bones and teeth contain 99% of all of the calcium in your body. The remaining one percent helps with blood clotting, contraction, and relaxation of muscles (including your heart muscle), transmission of nerve impulses, activation of enzymes and hormone secretion. A good source for calcium is milk, yogurt, cheese, and other dairy products. Also, dried beans, peas, and green vegetables. Mineral water may contribute a little calcium to your diet, as does hard water.

Chromium: Chromium is a mineral that is part of the glucose tolerance factor that regulates the actions of insulin. In chromium deficient people, insulin does not function properly. In such cases, chromium supplements can improve the body's ability to handle glucose. Experts believe that a chromium deficit is widespread, particularly among older people and may explain why the incidence of glucose intolerance increases with age. Brewer's yeast and wheat germ are rich in chromium. Other sources include whole grains, meats, cheeses, broccoli, and eggs.

Copper: A mineral that is in the body in small amounts, copper helps your body absorb and use iron and helps form hemoglobin and collagen. Some of the sources of copper include shellfish, liver, dried peas and beans, nuts, cocoa, fruits, and vegetables.

Germanium: Germanium is mineral not stored in your body, so 100% of what is taken in is excreted within two or three days. It can be found in garlic and ginseng. The benefits include improving mental alertness, lower blood pressure, anti-inflammatory, fight infect-ions, suppress tumors and boost your immune system.

Iron: Most of your body's iron resides in the hemoglobin of red blood cells, hemoglobin carries oxygen to your cells and transports carbon dioxide from your cells. Iron is also essential to enzymes involved in energy release, cholesterol metabolism, immunity, and connective-tissue production. Good sources of iron include liver and other meats, whole grains, shellfish, green leafy vegetables, and nuts.

Magnesium: Magnesium plays a role in protein synthesis, muscle relaxation and energy release. It also triggers important metabolic reactions, including calcium metabolism. It is found in most foods, particularly green leafy vegetables.

Potassium: Potassium plays an important role in maintaining the water balance in your body. It is crucial in the transmission of messages from your nerves to your muscles. It also acts as a catalyst in carbohydrate and protein metabolism. Bananas and melons are excellent sources for potassium, as well as legumes, meat, potatoes, prunes, Bok Choy and even yogurt.

Selenium: Selenium functions as an antioxidant. It helps prevent cell damage from free-radicals that form when oxygen attacks or oxidizes, fats and other compounds. Selenium supports your immune system, helping it to function at optimum as well as having antiviral properties. The Brazil nut is such a super source of selenium, it is recommended that you do not eat too many at a time. Other less potent sources are meat and fish.

Zinc: Zinc aids in the metabolism of carbohydrates, fats, and proteins. It is also part of the hormone insulin, helping transport vitamin A from its storage site in your liver to where it is used in your body. Zinc boosts your immune system. Oysters contain more zinc than any other food. Meat, poultry, eggs, and liver are also rich sources. Two servings of animal protein daily provide most of the zinc a healthy person needs.

(Herbs)

Aloe Vera: Aloe Vera is re-known for its wound healing effects. Many people keep an aloe plant in their kitchen, so it is readily available to treat burns from grease splatter or hot utensils. Aloe Vera is even safe for use by children. It can also help with the treatment of eczema, dandruff, acne, ringworm, gum disease, poison oak and poison ivy. Although Aloe Vera juice is marketed for oral consumption, with the claim that it relieves gastrointestinal complaints such as indigestion, these claims have not been proven. Use caution using it as a laxative, since your body can easily become addicted to it. I personally feel it would be wise to limit Aloe Vera to external use, particularly if you're pregnant, nursing a baby, or have one of the following conditions: gastritis, heartburn, kidney. disorders, irritable bowel syndrome, intestinal obstruction, ulcerative colitis, Chhorn's disease, hemorrhoids, or menstrual disorders.

Bilberry: With its potent antioxidant activity

Bilberry protects your body tissues, particularly blood vessels, from oxidizing agents circulating in your blood. Bilberry extracts may also reduce any tingling sensations in the extremities associated with diabetes. Several studies have shown that bilberry extracts stimulate blood vessels to release a substance that helps dilate veins and arteries. Bilberries help keep platelets from clumping together which thins the blood, prevents clotting, and improves circulation. Although both the fruit and leaves can be ingested, the leaves contain chemicals that irritate your liver if used for an extended period of time.

Black Cohosh: Black Cohosh acts as an anti-spasmodic to muscles, nerves, and blood vessels and as a muscle anti-inflammatory. This herb also helps to increase estrogen activity. Black cohosh can be a mild stomach tonic since its sweet and bitter flavors stimulate digestion. Early physicians also used black cohosh for serious infectious diseases including whooping cough, scarlet fever, and smallpox. People who cannot take aspirin should not take black cohosh. Since this herb may

promote blood flow to your head, it is possible you could experience dizziness.

Burdock: The roots and seeds of the Burdock plant are used widely in herbal medicine to support your liver function and as a cleansing botanical. Burdock roots stimulate digestion secretions, aiding in digestion. Burdock may also be useful in treating a variety of skin conditions, including acne and dryness. Burdock contains a starch-like substance called insulin that is easily digested. Burdock has been recommended to people with diabetes because studies show insulin is easier for them to metabolize than other starches. Insulin breaks down into the simple sugar fructose, which does not require insulin to move into cells. If you have ulcers, an irritable bowel or excessive stomach acid, burdock may worsen your condition.

Chamomile: Chamomile is widely used to treat gynecologic complaints. It has been found to contain strong antispasmodic and anti-inflammatory properties and is particularly effective in treating stomach and intestinal cramps. Chamomile also relieves excessive gas and bloating in your intestines as well as helping to relieve irritable bowel syndrome, nausea, and stomach flu. Chamomile has an excellent calming property and is often used as a sleep aid. Most people tolerate chamomile well, but if you have an allergy to ragweed you may want to think twice about using it.

Comfrey: Comfrey has been found to cause cells to divide at an increased rate, thus, healing your wounds more quickly. Comfrey may be used topically on cuts, bruises, abrasions, and burns. Since the internal use of comfrey has been under debate since cases of poisoning and even one death, due to comfrey ingestion, have been documented after long term use, would recommend that you reserve it for external purposes only.

Dandelion: The greens of the dandelion have been used as a diuretic. The roots contain insulin and laevulin, which are starch-like substances that my help balance your blood sugar, as well as a bitter substance that stimulates digestion. Dandelion leaves are rich in minerals and vitamins, particularly calcium and vitamins A, C, K and B-2. Dandelion roots are also used as a detoxifier and colon cleanser, with only rare instances of intestinal irritation, when used properly

Dong Quai: Dong Quai is also called Angelica Sinensis it is primarily used to treat menstrual complaints. Studies have shown that Dong Quai is useful in treating, infertility, premenstrual syndrome, menstrual problems such as cramping and irregular cycles, chronic miscarriages, and menopausal complaints. It is considered quite safe to use but may make some people's skin more sensitive to sun light.

Echinacea: Echinacea is well known for its antibiotic properties, it is one of the first things people reach for when they get a cold. It is also used today to help treat cancer, chronic fatigue syndrome, and aids. Although it was once considered unsafe to use echinacea for more than thirty days straight, it is now believed that it is quite safe with the only drawback being that it may mask the symptoms of a more serious underlying disease.

Fennel: Fennel is a great digestive aid as well

as an aid to diminishing gas in your intestines. Early physicians often used it as a tonic for colic in infants. As an antispasmodic, fennel acts on the smooth muscle of your respiratory passages as well as your stomach and intestines, which is the reason that fennel preparations are used to relieve bronchial spasms. Fennel is also known to have an estrogenic effect and has long been used to promote milk production in nursing mothers. Although a few rare individuals experience allergic reactions to fennel, it is generally considered safe and non-toxic.

Feverfew: Feverfew is used to relieve headaches, particularly vascular headaches such as migraines. Although some herbalists believe feverfew is most effective when used long-term to prevent chronic migraines, some people find it helpful when taken at the onset of a headache. Besides vascular headaches, feverfew may also benefit those who experience premenstrual head-aches, which are often due to fluid retention and hormonal effects. It is also reported to reduce fever and inflammation in joints and tissues. Feverfew can cause stomach upset and should not be used during pregnancy because it could promote a miscarriage.

Ginkgo: Ginkgo is reported to improve your circulation and as well as the vascular integrity in your head, heart, and extremities. It promotes increased neurotransmitters in your brain. Please note: Because Ginkgo promotes circulation in your head, it may worsen headaches. Large quantities of ginkgo can cause irritability, restlessness, diarrhea and nausea or vomiting.

Ginseng: Ginseng stimulates and strengthens your central nervous system in cases of fatigue, physical exertion, weakness from disease and injury and prolonged emotional stress. It is reported to help control diabetes, improve blood pressure, and heart action and reduce mental confusion, headaches, and weakness among the elderly. Ginseng also helps boost your immune system and fight cancer. Use of ginseng is not recommended if you have high blood pressure.

Goldenseal: Goldenseal has strong astringent

and anti-inflammatory properties which make it useful for treating conditions of your throat, stomach, and vagina when these tissues are inflamed, swollen or infected. It makes a good antiseptic skin wash for wounds and for internal skin surfaces such as in the vagina and ear canal. Because of its antibacterial effects, goldenseal can impair the beneficial bacteria of our digestive tracts the way that pharmaceutical antibiotics can. When taking goldenseal for long periods of time, you should supplement your body with acidophilus.

Horsetail: Horsetail is used to treat bladder infections and bladder weakness, such as occasional nocturnal incontinence. It helps with edema in your legs as well. Since horsetail contains silica and minerals, it is often used to strengthen bone, hair, and fingernails. Although there are no documented reported side effects or toxicity, that I am aware of, some believe that kidney irritation and interference with normal vitamin B1 metabolism could occur with long term, repetitive and frequent use.

Lavender: Lavender calms your nervous system. It has a mild sedating action and is also a weak antispasmodic for muscular tension. Lavender may also alleviate gas and bloating in your intestines. It has been found to relax bronchial passages, reducing inflammatory and allergic reactions, which is why Lavender is sometimes included in asthma, cough, and other respiratory formulas. Some people dislike the smell of lavender and find it nauseating or irritating to their nose.

Licorice: Licorice is used to soothe coughs and reduce inflammation, soothe, and heal ulcers and stomach inflammations, control blood sugar and balance hormones. Licorice is great for healing canker sores and cold sores. It is a potent antiviral agent and can be used to treat flu, herpes, and other viruses. Licorice is also a strong anti-inflammatory agent. Licorice may raise blood pressure in people who have hypertension. Very high doses may cause bloating and fluid retention therefore it should be avoided during pregnancy.

Milk Thistle: Milk Thistle is a potent anti-

oxidant and is used to detoxify your liver and metabolize harmful substances. It is used to treat liver disorders including cirrhosis. Other than a laxative effect, milk thistle is considered safe to take.

Passion Flower: Flower Passion Flower is

used for anxiety, insomnia, rest-less-ness, epilepsy, and other conditions of hyperactivity as well as high blood pressure. In Europe the flowers are added to numerous pharmaceuticals to treat nerve disorders, heart palpitations, anxiety, and high blood pressure. Although it is a strong pain reliever, it is not addictive. Even so, if you take large amounts of passion flower for an extended period, depression of your nervous system may result in fatigue and mental fogginess. I suggest that you start with a low dose, several times a day and increase as you learn how you respond to it.

Peppermint: Peppermint is widely used as a food flavoring and disinfectant. It is a tasty way to relieve gas, nausea, and stomach pain due to an irritable bowl, intestinal cramps, or indigestion. It is also used topically for the cooling and relaxing effect it has on your skin and has analgesic, antiseptic, antispasmodic, and decongestant effects. Although some people are allergic to peppermint, it is known to be a safe herb and is often used with children and infants.

St. John's Wort: St John's Wart has long

been used as an anti-inflammatory for strains, sprains, and contusions. It has also been used to treat muscular spasms, cramps and tension that results in muscular spasms. It is reported to relieve anxiety and tension and to act as an antidepressant. With long term use, it may make your skin more sensitive to sunlight. Please note: People have died as a result of not telling their doctor that they were taking St. John's Wart prior to being anesthetized for surgery.

Saw Palmetto: Saw Palmetto has long been considered an aphrodisiac and sexual rejuvenator, although little research supports this claim. It does, however, act on your sexual organs and many herbalists value it as a treatment for impotence and prostate enlargement. Because it can strengthen your urinary organs, Saw Palmetto is recommended to treat weakening urinary organs and the resulting incontinence that may occur in elderly people or women after menopause. It is also recommended for treating kidney stones. There have been no side effects reported with this herb that I am aware of.

Thyme: You can drink thyme tea for relief from coughs, bronchitis, and common colds (combining thyme with licorice or mint improves the flavor) Thyme has a pronounced effect on your respiratory system and in addition to fighting infections, it dries mucous membranes and relaxes spasms of bronchial passages, thus helping coughs, bronchitis, emphysema, and asthma. Its drying effect makes it useful to reduce the abundant watering of your eyes and nose associated with hay fever and other allergies. Thyme also combats parasites, such as hookworms and tapeworms, within your digestive tract as well as treats yeast infections. Although there are no known side effects with thyme teas and tinctures, very large dosages such as three or four cups of thyme tea consumed all at once may occasionally promote nausea and a sensation of warmth and perspiration.

Uva Ursi: This herb is disinfecting and promotes urine flow. It is especially recommended to treat illnesses cause by E. coli. Use it for chronic irritation, pain, mucus production and weakness of urinary organs. Some people are sensitive to this herb and have been poisoned by large amounts of 1/1/2 ounces or more.

Valerian: Valerian relieves anxiety and relaxes muscles. Although it is an excellent sedative and hypnotic, despite what some people have come to believe, valerian is not the source of the drug Valium. It's useful in simple cases of stress, anxiety, and nervous tension as well as more severe cases of hysteria, nervous twitching, hyperactivity, heart palpitations, tension head-aches and insomnia. Valerian occasion-ally has the opposite effect and may stimulate instead of sedate. When used for insomnia, in rare cases, valerian can cause morning grogginess. Reducing the dosage usually alleviates the problem. Valerian occasionally causes headaches and heart palpitations, when taken in large dosages of multiple droppers full of tincture or 4 or more cups of tea per day. It's advisable not to drive or operate machinery until you are familiar with how your body responds to Valerian.

Witch Hazel: The bark leaves and twigs of Witch Hazel are all high in tannins, giving this plant astringent properties. Although widely used on skin, its abilities to shrink swollen tissue makes it appropriate to treat laryngitis as well and a throat gargle of herbal (not drug store which is often mixed with isopropyl alcohol) witch hazel, myrrh and cloves reduces the pain of an uncomfortable sore throat. Witch hazel is sometimes used for symptoms of irritable bowel syndrome or colitis. If taken too frequently or in too large a dose, you may develop nausea.

DEVELOPING A DIET PLAN that will serve the needs of your physical body is vital if you want to maintain it at optimum, as is proper exercise and water. Please remember, when selecting your foods that digestion beings in your mouth. When you chew your food and mix it with the alkaline juices of your saliva, an enzyme called ptyalin begins to work. Carbohydrates start their digestion in your mouth. By the time they reach your stomach, they should be in a crystalline sugar form. The enzymes in your stomach are not prepared to break down any carbohydrates in a manner equivalent to the enzymes in your mouth. Therefore, if you do not chew your food well prior to swallowing and mix it properly with your saliva, you may find yourself gaining some weight, as a result of improperly digested carbohydrates in your stomach being stored as fat. This philosophy also applies to your liquid drinks. There is a saying, "Chew your drinks and swallow your food." This basically means that you should make sure whatever you are ingesting has properly commingled with your saliva prior to swallowing.

Your stomach is where the proteins you ingest begin their process of digestion. Hydrochloric acid goes after the fat and activates the enzyme pepsin. As the hydrochloric acid combines with other substances in your stomach to convert the fat lipids, the pepsin softens and begins to break down the protein into amino acids.

When the carbohydrates, fats and proteins reach your small intestines, they should already be turned into nutrients. These nutrients, including water-soluble vitamins and minerals, enter your blood stream and are distributed throughout your body for nourishment.

The last stage of your digestion is where the

byproducts of the nutrients and the waste products that your body does not need are eliminated. This process of elimination is done through breathing, perspiring, urinating and bowel movements.

It is important that you have the appropriate enzymes in your body to aid in proper digestion, since lack of proper digestion can cause more than simply heartburn. Other side effects are lack of energy, nervous tension, depression, lack of luster in your hair and skin, bloating, gas, stomach aches, ulcers, sleeplessness, weight gain and leaky gut; just to name a few. If you feel that you are not balancing your diet to accommodate proper digestive enzyme assistance, enzyme supplements are readily available in most supermarket and health food stores. The most common enzyme supplement is the papaya enzyme.

It is also important that you intake a sufficient amount of fiber each day to keep your elimination system in good working order. Constipation is very common in low fiber diets and is far more serious than most people think. If the waste products are not properly eliminated from your colon, they begin to harden, and toxins build up. This is called autointoxication and is when your body is literally poisoning itself. If your colon is not properly functioning, the toxic residue will be re-absorbed into your body. Your body will then attempt to use its secondary organs of elimination, such as your skin. Often times rashes are the by-products of a poorly functioning colon. Some symptoms of auto-intoxication are headaches, joint pain, stomach pains and acne. I'm sure if you investigate further, you'll discover many more.

If you suspect or know you are constipated a colon cleansing, followed by an increased fiber in your diet, will rectify it.

Your liver is a primary organ that needs to be maintained and cleansed regularly, since it is the filter of your body. As you grow, the pesticides and other toxic additives that are in your food, water and air enter your body, go into your blood stream and inevitably, at some point, go through your liver and your liver takes action. If it is taking in the toxin faster than it can process and eliminate it, a toxic buildup will eventually occur. A simple thing like drinking fresh lemon in water in the morning and taking flaxseed oil will do wonders for aiding your liver in cleansing itself.

*Note: Flaxseed oil is best assimilated when taken with food.

I have proved a few recipes to give you an idea of how to combine your foods to better improve your health and mood. This will give you a jump start for either selecting your own recipes or creating a few new ones!

DELICIOUS RECIPIES FOR BODY MAINTENANCE

*NOTE: WHENEVER POSSIBLE, use organic foods

Shoo-Flu Chicken Soup

This is a hearty stew-like soup that will build your immune system as well as satisfy your hunger.

FOR STOCK

1-whole chicken

2-quarts filtered water

1-medium onion

4-clove garlic (chopped or pressed)

1"- fresh ginger (sliced or grated)

4-6- cloves

1-stick cinnamon (or 1/4 tsp ground)

Salt & Pepper to taste

SOUP INGREDIENTS

2-4 - sliced carrots

1/8- cup sweet peas

1/4 - cup string beans

1/4 - cup mushrooms

1/4- cup cauliflower

1/4- cup broccoli

1/8- cup whole kernel corn

1/4 - cup rice (optional)

Place all of stock ingredients together in a large pot and bring to a boil. Reduce to simmer until the chicken is falling off the bone and the bones are almost soft. Scoop the chicken out of the pot and let it cool enough to allow you to pull the chicken meat off and put it back in the pot. If you do not want to keep the ginger pieces or the cloves in the stock, now is the time to remove them. (I keep them in because I enjoy their taste and texture). Add your vegetables and allow it to cook on low until the vegetables are tender.

Carrot & Ginger Coconut Soup.

Besides tasting great, the carrot is full of beta-carotene and the ginger will rev up your immune system. The coconut is believed to be good for your thyroid function.

1-pound carrots

2" - fresh ginger - (sliced or grated)

2 c. reduced fat coconut milk

1 c. pine nuts (for garnish)

Salt and pepper to taste

Cover carrots and ginger with water and bring to boil. Cook until all but 1/4" of the water is reduced (be careful not to burn!). Blend the cooked carrots and ginger in a food processor or a blender until they are a smooth paste and then return to the pan. Add the coconut milk and bring to a simmer.

When you are serving, garnish the soup with toasted pine nuts.

* Toasted Pine Nuts: Place pine nuts on a baking sheet and lightly coat with olive oil (if you have a spray oil it is best) Bake until golden brown. NOTE: Some people prefer to bake dry, but this will alter the flavor.

Beet Soup

This yummy soup can be served hot or cold. It is full of fiber and great for cleaning your liver.

4- large beets, peeled and chopped

4- cups water

4- cups beef broth

1- large onion, peeled, quartered

4- carrots, peeled, chopped

1- large potato, peeled, cut into 1/2-inch cubes

2 -cups thinly sliced cabbage

3/4- cup chopped fresh dill

3- Tbsp red wine vinegar

1- cup sour cream

Salt and pepper to taste

Place all of the ingredients except the vinegar and sour cream and 1/4 c. dill in a large pot and bring to a boil. Reduce to simmer and cook until the vegetables are tender. Now add the vinegar

Ladle soup into bowls. Top with sour cream and remaining 1/4 cup dill.

Cucumber Salad

This is not only makes a nice snack, but it is good for your heart but will act as a mild diuretic.

3 medium cucumbers, thinly sliced

1 medium sweet onion, sliced thin and separated into rings

1 cup white vinegar

1/4 cup vegetable oil

1 cup water

1/4 cup sugar, or more to taste (or diet sweetener)

The cucumbers may be scored, or part of the skin can be peeled for better absorption of the juice. Layer cucumbers with the onion in a large bowl. In a separate bowl, mix remaining ingredients, stirring until sugar has dissolved. Taste and adjust sugar for sweetness, adding more sugar, if needed. Pour over vegetables and toss lightly. Cover and chill for 2-4 hours before serving.

STRESSORS

I BEGAN THIS BOOK WITH the topic of stress and stressors and I now end it with the same. Stressors on your body play such a vital role in your health. You have learned some ways to manage them and allow, or not allow, them to affect you in all areas of your life. Our society has taught us certain belief systems that also render us vulnerable to stress. One of them is the concept of time.

What time is it anyway? Does anyone really know what time it is? The truth is that time was made up. Time, as we know it is completely artificial. That is one of the reasons, for those of you who get spiritual or psychic readings, it is so difficult for the reader to give you proper and accurate timing on anticipated events.

Do you seem to be always racing the clock or looking for more time? You are not alone. Most of society is suffering the same plight. In the 1950's we all got excited about the technology coming out. It was going to create a world where we would have more leisure time available to us for fun activities. That was a marvelous concept, do not you think? The problem was going to be finding enough activities to keep us active and alert because of this extra time we would have available. Work would be simplified and therefore was going to take up a very small percentage of our day and the fear of becoming bored was our biggest concern.

Instead, most people find they have not any time to do anything. You are in a mad rush to get to work, complete the job, drive the children here and there, cook the family (or yourself) dinner, etc. You watch the clock wistfully in hopes of grabbing just a small bit of time for yourself. Technology has not liberated you at all; so, what to do?

Only you can make that shift. I have already covered points on getting organized and remaining calm in situations.

I have also covered foods and supplements and how they come into play; but what about sleep? How much sleep are you getting?

Sleep is an essential component for your well-being. Before society had all of those clocks telling you what time it was and when you should sleep vs. when you should wake, it is believed that most people slept around ten hours every night. Now we are lucky to find people who manage to fit in eight hours of sleep per night. Studies have shown that people who sleep eight hours per night find they are more productive and more energetic and feel better once they begin sleeping ten hours every night. So, for those of you who are getting less than eight hours of sleep each night, wouldn't it make sense for you to try to shoot for a little more sleep?

If you think that you can make up for the sleep you lose during the week on the weekend by sleeping in and this will somehow balance things out, think again. What you are doing is creating a disruptive sleeping pattern and could eventually end up with insomnia.

It is important to avoid stimulants that will activate your sympathetic nervous system into preparing you for the flight or fight syndrome if you want to combat stress and have a deep, restful sleep. Coffee, tea, and chocolate are among this group. If you are ingesting any of these at bedtime, it is bound to have an effect on the quality of your rest.

Noises interrupt your sleep even if you're sleeping through them. It is a very bad habit to sleep with your television on. If you insist you can't fall asleep if it is not on, then invest in a timer and set it. When you are sleeping, you are feeding data into your subconscious, so if you do not want to invest in a timer and insist on falling asleep with the television on, at least take the time to select a station with suitable shows playing for your subconscious to absorb. I suggest that if you do feel the need for a little noise to sleep by, you select a CD or tape containing some soothing music, or even a foreign language or other study that you are interested in.

Lack of adequate exercise can make it difficult to sleep as well, but it is recommended you do not exercise before bedtime. Your body will say sleep, but your oxygen filled mind is apt to be in high gear. As I mentioned earlier, we are all working within a schedule, so if your schedule only allows you to exercise at night then try some breathing techniques for relaxation, meditation, or soothing music if you find that you are too wound up to sleep.

If you are sleeping well at night, the next step is to nap. Interestingly, it is not recommended for those of you who have poor night sleep habits, as it is believed to only make things worse. But a nice nap in the middle of the afternoon, if you don't want to meditate, is a terrific addition to your sleeping repertoire. Men seem to be better at power naps than women. A power nap by definition is ten minutes or less. A good nap, however, lasts between twenty and thirty minutes. This "down time" does a world of good for your body. Some believe it helps lengthen your life span. You may go into a slumber, light doze, or simply rest. But try to take the down time whenever possible, you'll be glad you did.

I mentioned coffee and tea as being detrimental to your sleeping pattern, but let's take a closer look at them; since they can also be detrimental to your overall health, and therefore a powerful stressor if taken incorrectly.

Most of the negative effects of caffeine are not a concern with an occasional user, but with regular use of over one hundred milligrams daily, it could pose cause for you to sit up and take notice. The average cup of coffee has 120-150 mg. of caffeine. Tea has 50-60 mg. of caffeine, and cola has 30-65 mg. of caffeine. A total intake of 500 mg. of caffeine daily is considered high. This would include caffeine derived from coffee, tea, soda, chocolate, or drugs. It is hard to believe that the very thing you rely upon to pick you up and get you going could actually be bringing you down and making you depressed, or even ill.

The following is a list of the most common negative effects (stressors) caffeine can have on your body:

Nervousness, irritability, insomnia, "restless legs," dizziness, and fatigue

Headaches

Heartburn

Anxiety

Hyperactivity

Bed wetting in children who consume caffeine (remember it is in chocolate and most soda)

Increased acidity in stomach

Loss of minerals such as potassium, magnesium, and zinc.

Loss of vitamins including the B vitamins, particularly thiamin, loss of vitamin C

Reduced absorption of iron and calcium- especially if consumed around mealtimes

Osteoporosis and anemia

Interruption of growth in children and adolescents

Diarrhea

Increased blood pressure and hypertension

Increased cholesterol and triglycerides blood levels

Heart rhythm disturbances and mild arrhythmia palpitations

Increased risk of heart attacks

Fibrocystic breast disease

Birth defects and miscarriages

Kidney stones

Increased incidence of certain cancers, including bladder cancer, ovarian cancer and

pancreatic cancer

Prostate enlargement

Hypoglycemia

If you are concerned about the stress and

negative effects the food you are putting in your body may be having on it, take some time to read the labels before you purchase them.

If you use the information in this book as a guideline for your daily routine for both physical and body maintenance, you will eventually enjoy a better quality of living that has limited amounts of stress.

There is one more factor that I'd like to mention before I end this book. That is the necessity to stay flexible. Everything in life changes; if you are not willing to go with the flow, you are bound to be left behind. Complete seminars have been created on just this topic alone. Inability to be flexible has cost many a company/person a powerful future. Be willing to change, move ahead, and improve; while being flexible, remember to stay positive. The glass is either half empty or half full, the choice is yours. Positive reinforcement through affirmations can help you to shift more comfortably through the changes that occur in your life. Your emotions play an intricate part of the scope of who you are, but they are in no means the ultimate of who you are. You are able to control, change and shift them at will. This is an important factor to remember, since your emotional body does affect your health, both mentally and physically. Recognizing this fact, you can now understand the possibility and often the necessity of reprogramming your thought process that you have developed over the years as is needed to accommodate the changes that area occurring in your life.

Stress indeed is a part of live, but it certainly does not have to be a way of life. Control stress instead of letting stress control you. Take back your power and smile, smile, smile!

ABOUT THE AUTHOR

BORN IN UPSTATE NEW York, Lena Sheehan (Also known as Eileen Sheehan) began her studies of holistic care of body, mind, and spirit in 1983. She now holds a diploma in Naturopathy, is a member of the American Association of Professional Hypnotherapists, a Certified Nutrition Specialist and has received certification in Emotional Release Therapy (ERT). She is a Reiki Mater Teacher (fifth generation from Mrs. Takata), a Karuna Ki Master and the founder of the Sheehan Technique of Healing. On the spiritual side of things, Lena is an ordained minister (1993) and a Director of Ministries for the Universal Brotherhood Movement (1995) and was ordained by Dr. Willard Fuller into the evangelistic ministry of the Lively Stones Fellowship in 2003. She is also a medical intuitive as well as a Spiritist, spiritual consultant and animal communicator.

Rev. Sheehan shares her knowledge and talents, not only with private clients for personal, business, and medical matters, but in occasional radio appearances, lectures, and workshops with groups such as Hospice and adult education classes at the local college. She has also created several distance courses and teaches a virtual class once a month.

Visit Lena on her website: www.lenainc.com[1]

1. http://www.lenainc.com

Books by Eileen Sheehan

[MOST ARE AVAILABLE in eBook, paperback & audio format]

[GENRE: PARANORMAL OMANCE/THRILLERS]

THE VAMPIRE, THE HANDLER, AND ME 5*Award Winner

FOR LOVE OF A VAMPIRE

THE PRINCESS AND THE VAMPIRE KING

A VAMPIRE'S LOVE Bronze Medal winner 2025

EMERGENCE

DRAGON LOVE 5*Award Winner

DREAM LOVE 5*Award Winner

GHOST LOVE

SISTERS

OF WOLVES AND MEN

ELIZA: THE AWAKENING

CONRY) 5*Award Winner

BEYOND THE VEIL OF TIME

Tugurlan Chronicles

VAMPIRE INIQUITY (Book 1) 5*Award Winner

THE CURE (Book 2)

VAMPIRES AND WEREWOLVES (Book 3)

Vampire Witch Trilogy

VAMPIRE WITCH (Book 1) 5*Award Winner plus Bronze Medal 2024

VAMPIRE QUEEN (Book 2)

KINGS & QUEENS (Book 3)

Shadow Love Duo

SHADOW LOVE: BOOK ONE

SHADOW LOVE: BOOK TWO

a Wolf Affair Trilogy

a WOLF AFFAIR (Book 1)

WOLF MOUNTAIN (Book 2)

MISSY'S CHOICE (Book 3)

The Adventures of Vickie Anderson

VICKIE: Doctor by day. Zombie hunter by night (Book 1) 5*Award Winner

VICKIE: Doctor by day. Werewolf hunter by night (Book 2)

VICKIE: Doctor by day. Ghost hunter by night (Book 3)

VICKIE: Doctor by day. Vampire medic by night (Book 4)

Kendra's Journey

WHERE ZOMBIES WALK (Book 1) 5*Award Winner

THE REGIME (Book 2)

CENTER LAND (Book 3)

ZOMBIES AND ALIENS (Book 4)

The Esmerelda Sleuth Series

THE OTHER SIDE OF THE MIRROR (Book 1) 5*Award Winner)

THE MAGIC BOX (Book 2)

BEYOND THE PORTAL (Book 3)

THE JOURNAL (Book 4)

Jasper Trilogy

JASPER: THE BEGINNING (Book 1)

JASPER: LOVE AND MONSTERS (Book 2)

JASPER: THE RECKONING (Book 3)

Blood Cure Trilogy

BLOOD CURE (Book 1)

THE RESCUE (Book 2)

THE ANNIHILATION (Book 3)

Aisling Trilogy

AISLING: In the Land of Wolves (Book 1) 5*Award Winner

AISLING: In the Land of Vampires (Book 2)

AISLING: Lighthouse Magic (Book 3)

AISLING: Changing Worlds (Book 4)

Enid Trilogy

ENID (Book 1)) 5*Award Winner

ENID (Book 2)

ENID (Book 3)

BOOKS BY AILENE FRANCES

[GENRE: ROMANCE]

LOVE MISUNDERSTOOD

(Historical Georgian Era Romance)

PAPER WIDOW 5*Award Winner

(Historical Western Romance)

LOVE AT WOLF CREEK 5*Award Winner

(Historical Western Romance)

FOR LOVE OR MONEY

(Contemporary Mid-Western Romance)

BOOKS BY E. F. SHEEHAN

[GENRE: ALTERNATIVE ROMANCE/DRAMA]

TOAST WITH JELLY

A Tragedy of a Lesbian Confused

BOOKS BY LENA SHEEHAN

[GENRE: SELF-HELP]

HUMAN, HELP THYSELF

Natural Solutions for Stress of Body, Mind & Spirit

BASIC HYPNOSIS

ALL ABOUT REIKI

www.ingramcontent.com/pod-product-compliance
Lightning Source LLC
LaVergne TN
LVHW041103150826
845673LV00007B/1900

* 9 7 9 8 2 2 4 1 4 6 4 8 2 *